101 Bizarre, Quirky and Totally Fun Adventures in the Midwest

Explore the Wonderful and Wacky Heartland of America!

Travel with Jack and Kitty

with
Kitty Norton

with
Jack Norton

Contents

Sign Up for Our Newsletter   v

1. Welcome to the Wonderfully Wacky Midwest   1
2. Illinois: The Prairie State's Peculiar Pleasures   5
3. Indiana: Hoosier State Oddities   14
4. Iowa: Hawkeye State Hidden Gems   25
5. Kansas: Sunflower State Surprises and Delights   34
6. Michigan: Great Lakes State Wonders and Oddities   44
7. Minnesota: Land of 10,000 Wacky Adventures   53
8. Missouri: Show-Me State Marvels and Curiosities   68
9. Nebraska: Cornhusker State Curiosities and Delights   78
10. North Dakota: Roughrider State Oddities and Adventures   88
11. Ohio: Buckeye State Oddities and Amusements   98

12. South Dakota: Mount Rushmore State Marvels and Mysteries   108
13. Wisconsin: Badger State Wonders and Oddities   118
14. The Road Goes Ever On   128
    About the Authors   134
    Connect with Jack and Kitty   136

Sign Up for Our Newsletter

Enjoy the BEST stories, news & jokes!

For more info, visit:

https://jackandkitty.com/free/

Chapter 1

Welcome to the Wonderfully Wacky Midwest

The Midwest is a region that often flies under the radar when it comes to travel destinations, but those who take the time to explore this incredible part of the United States are in for a delightful surprise. From the friendly faces and warm hospitality to the stunning natural beauty and rich cultural heritage, the Midwest has something to offer every type of traveler. But beyond the well-known attractions and tourist hotspots lies a world of quirky, bizarre, and utterly unforgettable adventures that will leave you amazed, amused, and eager to discover more.

That's where this book comes in. 101 Bizarre, Quirky and Totally Fun Adven-

Travel with Jack and Kitty tures in the Midwest is your ultimate guide to uncovering the hidden gems and offbeat attractions that make the Midwest truly unique. Whether you're a lifelong resident looking for new places to explore or a curious traveler seeking an authentic and immersive experience, this book will take you on a journey through the weird, wonderful, and wholly unexpected side of America's Heartland.

Inside these pages, you'll find 101 carefully curated adventures spread across 12 Midwestern states, each with its own distinct flavor and charm. From the world's largest ball of twine to mysterious sculptures, from a bizarre hair museum to an infinity room, this book is packed with destinations that will spark your imagination, challenge your perceptions, and leave you with unforgettable memories.

But this book is more than just a list of places to visit. Each entry is a mini-adventure in itself, with vivid descriptions, fascinating backstories, and insider tips to help you make the most of your experience. Whether you're a history buff, an art lover, a nature enthusiast, or just a curious soul, you'll find plenty of inspiration and infor-

101 Bizarre, Quirky and Totally Fun Adventures in ...

mation to fuel your wanderlust and guide your travels.

So how can you use this book to plan your own Midwestern adventure? The possibilities are endless, but here are a few suggestions to get you started:

1. Pick a state and explore all the quirky attractions it has to offer. Each chapter is dedicated to a different Midwestern state, so you can easily plan a road trip or weekend getaway around the destinations that interest you most.

2. Create a themed itinerary based on your interests. Are you a fan of outsider art? Love all things weird and wacky? You get the idea.

3. Use the book as a source of inspiration for your own adventures. Take the time to explore the small towns, back roads, and hidden corners of the Midwest, and you never know what kind of quirky and captivating attractions you might stumble upon.

No matter how you choose to use this book, one thing is certain: the Midwest is a region that will surprise you, delight you, and leave you wanting more. So grab your sense of adventure, your camera, and your love for the unexpected, and get ready to explore the wonderfully wacky side of

Travel with Jack and Kitty

America's Heartland. The quirky, bizarre, and totally fun adventures await!
Have a super day!
Jack and Kitty
Winona, Minnesota

Chapter 2

Illinois: The Prairie State's Peculiar Pleasures

Illinois, known as the Prairie State, is a land of diverse landscapes, vibrant cities, and a rich history that has shaped America. But beyond the skyscrapers of Chicago and the rolling hills of the countryside lies a treasure trove of quirky, bizarre, and utterly delightful adventures waiting to be discovered.

From a giant statue of Superman to a museum dedicated to the humble postcard, Illinois is full of surprises that will capture your imagination and leave you grinning from ear to ear. Join us as we explore eight of the most incredible and unusual hidden gems the Prairie State has to offer. Get ready to embrace your inner adventurer and uncover the peculiar pleasures that make Illinois truly unforgettable.

1. The Superman Statue (Metropolis, IL)

In the small town of Metropolis, Illinois, you'll find a sight that will make you believe a man can fly. Standing proudly in the town square is a 15-foot-tall bronze statue of Superman, complete with his iconic red cape and chiseled features.

The statue, erected in 1993, pays homage to the town's claim to fame as the official hometown of the Man of Steel. Visitors can pose for photos with the superhero, and even stop by the Super Museum next door to browse a collection of Superman memorabilia.

Every June, the town hosts the Superman Celebration, a festival that draws thousands of fans from around the world. With costume contests, celebrity guests, and a parade featuring the Man of Steel himself, it's a quirky and fun-filled event that will make you feel like a kid again.

101 Bizarre, Quirky and Totally Fun Adventures in ...

2. The Leaning Tower of Niles (Niles, IL)

No, your eyes aren't playing tricks on you. In the suburb of Niles, Illinois, you'll find a half-scale replica of the famous Leaning Tower of Pisa, complete with its distinctive tilt.

The tower, built in 1934 by industrialist Robert Ilg, was originally intended to hide water filtration tanks for a nearby swimming pool complex. Today, it stands as a beloved landmark and a testament to the creativity and eccentricity of its builder.

Visitors can climb to the top of the tower for a unique perspective on the surrounding area, and even enjoy a picnic in the adjacent park. The Leaning Tower of Niles is a whimsical and Instagram-worthy stop that will leave you marveling at the unexpected wonders of Illinois.

3. The Lizzadro Museum of Lapidary Art (Elmhurst, IL)

Prepare to be dazzled by the beauty and intricacy of gemstones and minerals at the Lizzadro Museum of Lapidary Art in Elmhurst. This one-of-a-kind museum showcases the art of cutting and polishing stones, with exhibits that range from ancient Chinese jade carvings to modern-day gemstone sculptures.

Marvel at the colorful displays of geodes, fossils, and petrified wood, and learn about the fascinating process of turning rough stones into sparkling works of art. The museum also offers hands-on activities and demonstrations, allowing visitors to try their hand at gem cutting and polishing.

Whether you're a geology enthusiast or simply appreciate the beauty of nature, the Lizzadro Museum of Lapidary Art is a hidden gem that will leave you enchanted and inspired.

4.The World's Largest Mailbox (Casey, IL)

Imagine strolling through the quaint streets of Casey, Illinois, when suddenly you come face-to-face with a mailbox so massive it could easily double as a small apartment. Standing at an impressive height, the World's Largest Mailbox is a sight to behold. But this gargantuan letterbox isn't just for show – it's fully functional!

If you're feeling adventurous, you can

climb the ladder attached to the side of the mailbox and drop your letter inside. Just be sure to bring a stamp big enough to match the size of this colossal creation. Just kidding!

As you stand in the shadow of this Guinness World Record-holding marvel, you can't help but wonder how the postal workers manage to collect the mail from such a towering structure. Perhaps they have a team of trained acrobats who scale the mailbox daily, or maybe they employ a fleet of drones to retrieve the letters from the top. Either way, sending a postcard from the World's Largest Mailbox is an experience you won't soon forget.

5. The World's Largest Wooden Shoes (Casey, IL)

If you thought the World's Largest Mailbox was impressive, wait until you feast your eyes on the World's Largest Wooden Shoes at Wildflour Bakery and Candy Company. These gargantuan clogs, weighing a staggering 5,000 pounds collectively, are a testament to the town's love for all things supersized.

As you approach the bakery, you'll be

greeted by the sight of these enormous wooden shoes, each one large enough to comfortably house a family of four. You might find yourself wondering what kind of giant could possibly wear such massive footwear – perhaps a friendly ogre with a sweet tooth for baked goods? Or maybe a family of elves who've taken up residence in the shoes, using them as a cozy cottage.

Whatever the case may be, one thing is for sure – these wooden shoes are a true marvel of craftsmanship and creativity. And if you're lucky, you might even catch a whiff of the delectable treats being whipped up inside the bakery, adding an extra layer of sweetness to your visit.

6. The Museum of the Grand Prairie (Mahomet, IL)

Step back in time and experience the rugged beauty and pioneer spirit of the Illinois prairie at the Museum of the Grand Prairie in Mahomet. This interactive museum brings the history of the region to life through engaging exhibits and hands-on activities.

Explore a replica of a 19th-century one-room schoolhouse, sit in a covered wagon, and try your hand at churning butter or grinding corn. Learn about the Indigenous people who called the prairie home, and discover the impact of the railroad on the settlement and growth of Illinois.

The museum also features a stunning collection of natural history specimens, including fossils, minerals, and preserved plants and animals. The Museum of the Grand Prairie is a fascinating and immersive experience that will leave you with a newfound appreciation for the hardy pioneers who shaped the state's history.

7. The Popeye Statue (Chester, IL)

Ahoy, mateys! In the river town of Chester, Illinois, you'll find a statue that will make you want to eat your spinach. Standing at an impressive 6 feet tall, the bronze sculpture of Popeye the Sailor Man pays tribute to the beloved cartoon character and his creator, Chester native E.C. Segar.

The statue, erected in 1977, stands in Segar Memorial Park, surrounded by other sculptures of Popeye's friends and foes, including Olive Oyl, Bluto, and Wimpy. Visitors can pose for photos with the muscular mariner and even visit the Popeye Museum next door to learn more about the history of the comic strip and its characters.

Every September, the town hosts the Popeye Picnic, a celebration of all things Popeye, with food, games, and a parade featuring everyone's favorite sailor. The Popeye Statue is a quirky and nostalgic stop that will bring a smile to your face and a spring to your step.

8. The Brookfield Zoo (Brookfield, IL)

Embark on a wild adventure at the Brookfield Zoo, one of the largest and most diverse zoos in the country. With over 450 species of animals from around the world, the zoo offers a chance to get up close and personal with nature's most fascinating creatures.

Walk through the lush tropical rainforest of the Tropic World exhibit, where you'll encounter gorillas, monkeys, and exotic birds. Watch the playful dolphins leap and splash in the Seven Seas underwater viewing area, and marvel at the majestic tigers and lions in the Big Cats exhibit.

The zoo also offers a variety of interac-

101 Bizarre, Quirky and Totally Fun Adventures in ...

tive experiences, such as giraffe feedings, penguin encounters, and a chance to pet stingrays in the shallow waters of the Stingray Bay. With its commitment to conservation and education, the Brookfield Zoo is a fun and meaningful destination for animal lovers of all ages.

* * *

From the whimsical charm of the Superman Statue to the wild wonders of the Brookfield Zoo, Illinois's quirky attractions offer a glimpse into the state's diverse culture, history, and natural beauty. These eight adventures are just a small sample of the many hidden gems waiting to be discovered in the Prairie State.

Whether you're a lifelong resident or a curious traveler, these peculiar pleasures will leave you with unforgettable memories and a newfound appreciation for Illinois's unique character. So, grab your sense of adventure, your camera, and your love for the unconventional, and set out to explore the weird and wonderful side of Illinois. You never know what delightful surprises await you in the heart of the Midwest!

Chapter 3

Indiana: Hoosier State Oddities

Indiana, affectionately known as the Hoosier State, is a land of small-town charm, rolling farmlands, and a rich cultural heritage. But beneath its unassuming exterior lies a treasure trove of quirky, bizarre, and utterly captivating adventures waiting to be discovered.

From a museum dedicated to the world's most famous ball to a giant shoe house, Indiana is full of surprises that will make you do a double-take and grin from ear to ear. Join us as we uncover eight of the most incredible and unusual hidden gems the Hoosier State has to offer. Get ready to embrace your inner curiosity and embark on a journey through the delightfully odd and endlessly entertaining side of Indiana.

101 Bizarre, Quirky and Totally Fun Adventures in ...

* * *

1. The RV/MH Hall of Fame and Museum (Elkhart, IN)

Rev up your engines and hit the road to the RV/MH Hall of Fame and Museum in Elkhart, Indiana. This one-of-a-kind museum showcases the history and evolution of recreational vehicles and manufactured homes, from the earliest horse-drawn campers to the sleek and modern RVs of today.

Step inside a vintage Airstream trailer, marvel at the intricate craftsmanship of a 1930s wooden travel trailer, and explore the unique designs of over 50 RVs and mobile homes on display. Learn about the pioneers of the RV industry and the impact of these homes on wheels on American culture and travel.

Whether you're a seasoned RV enthusiast or simply appreciate the ingenuity and nostalgia of these classic vehicles, the RV/MH Hall of Fame and Museum is a fascinating and fun-filled destination that will leave you itching to hit the open road.

2. The World's Largest Ball of Paint (Alexandria, IN)

In the small town of Alexandria, Indiana, you'll find a sight that will make you wonder, "How did they do that?" Behold the World's Largest Ball of Paint, a massive sphere covered in over 25,000 layers of paint and weighing in at a whopping 5,000 pounds.

The ball began as a simple baseball in 1977, when local resident Michael Carmichael started painting it as a fun project with his son. Over the years, the ball grew and grew, as visitors from around the world added their own layers of paint to the ever-expanding orb.

Today, the ball is housed in a custom-built barn, where visitors can add their own coat of paint and leave their mark on this quirky piece of Hoosier history. The World's Largest Ball of Paint is a testament to the power of persistence and the joy of creating something truly unique.

3. The Rotary Jail Museum (Crawfordsville, IN)

Get locked up in a piece of criminal history at the Rotary Jail Museum in Crawfordsville, Indiana. This unusual jail, built in 1882, features a unique rotating cell block design that allowed jailers to control the movement of prisoners with the turn of a hand crank.

Take a guided tour of the jail and learn about the ingenious but ultimately flawed design, which proved to be both escape-prone and inhumane. See the original cells, complete with their iron bars and stark furnishings, and imagine the lives of the prisoners who once called this place home.

The Rotary Jail Museum is a fascinating glimpse into the history of crime and punishment in America, and a reminder of the importance of prison reform and human rights. It's a thought-provoking and unforgettable experience that will leave you with a new perspective on justice and incarceration.

4. Old Ben (Kokomo, IN)

Old Ben, the world's largest steer, was born in 1902 and lived until 1910. At birth, he weighed an impressive 125 pounds, and by the time of his death, he had reached an astonishing weight of between 4,585 and 4,720 pounds. Standing at 6.5 feet tall and measuring 16.25 feet from nose to tail tip, Old Ben was a truly remarkable specimen.

Throughout his life, Old Ben's owners received numerous offers from circus owners and sideshow representatives who wanted to purchase the colossal steer. However, his owners declined all offers, preferring to showcase Old Ben themselves in a private tent at fairs throughout Indiana, including the State Fair for several years. In 1968, Old Ben was featured in Ripley's "Believe It Or Not," further cementing his status as a world-famous attraction.

Today, visitors to Kokomo, Indiana, can see Old Ben on display in a pavilion at Highland Park. The pavilion also houses the Giant Sycamore Stump, another fascinating natural wonder. Tourists interested in learning more about Old Ben's life and legacy can read his complete history online before visiting this unique attraction.

5. Harmonist Labryinth (New Harmony, IN)

New Harmony, Indiana, is home to a historic labyrinth that serves as a striking remnant of the Rappites, an ultra-religious German society that once sought to create a perfect community in the early 19th century. The labyrinth, originally designed as a place for meditation and reflection, symbolizes the Rappites' attempt to overcome life's challenges. Although the community ultimately disbanded due to a vow of celibacy, the labyrinth remains a testament to their unique history.

Visitors to New Harmony can explore the labyrinth, which was restored to its original form in 2008 after falling into disrepair and being temporarily converted into a maze in the 1930s. The labyrinth features a single path that winds through shrubs, leading to a central stone Rappite temple. Admission is free, and the site is open year-round. For those short on time or patience, gates provide a shortcut directly to the center.

In addition to the labyrinth, New Harmony has preserved many of the older buildings from its early communities. A stroll through the town offers visitors a glimpse into the workings of an early American religious utopia. The labyrinth is located on the main street that runs through New Harmony, making it easy to find and incorporate into your visit to this historic town.

6. Giant Santa (Evansville, IN)

Giant Santa, a 35-foot-tall statue, stands tall in Evansville, Indiana, a city located 40 miles west of the town of Santa Claus. The impressive figure was built in 1974 by local residents Doyle Kifer, Michael Talbert, and James Reynolds III, originally part of an "Enchanted World of Christmas" display at the Old Courthouse in Evansville. The display also featured a nearly-as-large King Kong climbing the building, adding a unique twist to the Christmas theme.

Over the years, Santa has been relocated several times, from Mesker Park near the zoo to Busler's Truck Stop, where he stood for more than two decades. However, by 2011, the truck stop had been demolished, and Santa's once-vibrant red suit had faded, giving him a somewhat unsettling appearance with his piercing blue eyes and flared nostrils. In 2012, the statue was moved to a junkyard, where he lay facedown and forgotten for several years.

In early 2016, local resident Ron McKeethen discovered the forgotten statue and initiated a crowdfunding campaign to "Stand Santa Back Up." With the support of the community and the Contingency of International Santas, Giant Santa was fully restored and erected at his current location on September 24, 2016. Visitors to Evansville can now find the towering Santa statue standing proudly at 11812 US Hwy 41, on the southbound side at the intersection of Old State Rd, just 7.5 miles north of downtown Evansville. A time capsule has been placed inside the statue to preserve his unique history for future generations.

7. The Bluespring Caverns (Bedford, IN)

Descend into a subterranean wonderland at the Bluespring Caverns in Bedford, Indiana. These stunning caverns, formed over millions of years by the flowing waters of the Lost River, feature over 21 miles of explored passages and a host of incredible geological formations.

Take a guided boat tour through the caverns and marvel at the towering stalactites, shimmering pools, and eerie underwater caves. Learn about the unique ecosystem of the caverns, which is home to a variety of rare and endangered species, including blind cavefish and albino crayfish.

The Bluespring Caverns are a natural wonder that will leave you in awe of the beauty and mystery of the underground world. It's an unforgettable adventure that will remind you of the incredible diversity and resilience of life on our planet.

8. The World's Largest Egg (Mentone, IN)

In the small town of Mentone, Indiana, you'll find a sight that will make you crack a smile. Standing at over 10 feet tall and weighing in at over 3,000 pounds, the World's Largest Egg is a true wonder of roadside Americana.

The egg, which is made of concrete and painted a gleaming white, was originally built in the 1940s as a symbol of the town's

101 Bizarre, Quirky and Totally Fun Adventures in ...

thriving egg industry. Today, it stands as a beloved landmark and a reminder of the importance of agriculture and community pride in rural America.

Visitors can take photos with the giant egg, and even visit the nearby Mentone Egg Festival, which features egg-themed games, contests, and plenty of delicious egg dishes. The World's Largest Egg is a quirky and charming attraction that will leave you with a newfound appreciation for the simple joys of small-town life.

* * *

From the towering RV/MH Hall of Fame to the subterranean wonders of the Bluespring Caverns, Indiana's quirky attractions offer a glimpse into the state's diverse culture, history, and natural beauty. These eight adventures are just a small sample of the many hidden gems waiting to be discovered in the Hoosier State.

Whether you're a lifelong resident or a curious traveler, these oddities and adventures will leave you with unforgettable memories and a newfound appreciation for Indiana's unique character. So, grab your sense of adventure, your camera, and your love for the unconventional, and set out to explore the weird and wonderful side of Indiana. You never know what delightful surprises await you in the heart of the Midwest!

Chapter 4

Iowa: Hawkeye State Hidden Gems

Iowa, the heart of the Heartland, is a state that often flies under the radar when it comes to quirky and unique attractions. However, beneath its unassuming exterior lies a treasure trove of bizarre, fun, and totally unforgettable adventures waiting to be explored.

From a museum dedicated to the world's most famous airplane to a massive wooden nickel and a shoe tree, Iowa is full of surprises that will delight and amuse visitors of all ages. Join us as we uncover eight of the most incredible and unusual hidden gems the Hawkeye State has to offer. Get ready to embrace your inner curiosity and discover a side of Iowa you never knew existed.

1. The World's Largest Wooden Nickel (Iowa City, IA)

Step back in time and marvel at the World's Largest Wooden Nickel in Iowa City. This gigantic replica, measuring 16 feet in diameter, was created in 2006 to commemorate the 150th anniversary of the Iowa State Bank.

Made from wood salvaged from a 19th-century railroad bridge, the nickel is a testament to the ingenuity and creativity of the local community. Visitors can admire the intricate details of the carving, which includes the bank's name, the anniversary dates, and the iconic image of a bison.

Take a photo with this one-of-a-kind roadside attraction and learn about the history of currency and commerce in the United States. The World's Largest Wooden Nickel is a quirky and educational stop that will leave you with a newfound appreciation for the power of a simple coin.

2. The Grotto of the Redemption (West Bend, IA)

Discover a hidden gem of spiritual beauty and human perseverance at the Grotto of the Redemption in West Bend. This awe-inspiring shrine, built over a period of 42 years by Father Paul Dobberstein, is the world's largest man-made grotto.

Wander through the nine separate grottos, each depicting a scene from the life of Jesus Christ. Marvel at the intricate mosaics and sculptures, created from precious stones, gems, and minerals from around the world. The attention to detail and the sheer scale of the project are a testament to Father Dobberstein's faith and dedication.

The Grotto of the Redemption is a peaceful and contemplative space that offers visitors a chance to reflect and find solace. Whether you're a person of faith or simply appreciate the beauty of art and architecture, this hidden gem is a must-see destination in Iowa.

3. The Shoe Tree (Milford, IA)

Take a drive down Highway 71 near Milford and keep your eyes peeled for an unusual sight: a towering cottonwood tree adorned with hundreds of shoes. This quirky roadside attraction, known as the Shoe Tree, has been a local landmark for over 30 years.

The origins of the Shoe Tree are shrouded in mystery, but legend has it that a pair of newlyweds got into an argument on their honeymoon and threw their shoes into the tree. Since then, countless travelers have added their own footwear to the branches, creating a colorful and eclectic display.

Take a moment to admire the variety of shoes, from worn-out work boots to glittery high heels, and ponder the stories behind each pair. If you're feeling adventurous, toss your own shoes into the tree and become part of the legend. The Shoe Tree is a whimsical and lighthearted stop that celebrates the quirkiness . of small-town America.

4. The Hobo Museum (Britt, IA)

Step into the fascinating world of America's nomadic workers at the Hobo Museum in Britt. This unique museum, located in the "Hobo Capital of the World," showcases the history and culture of hobos, tramps, and railroad workers who rode the rails in search of work and adventure.

Explore exhibits that feature authentic hobo artifacts, such as handmade tools, clothing, and artwork. Learn about the hobo code of ethics, the secret symbols used to communicate with other travelers, and the impact of the Great Depression on the hobo way of life.

The museum also hosts the annual Hobo Convention, a gathering of modern-day hobos and enthusiasts who celebrate the spirit of freedom and camaraderie. Whether you're a history buff or simply curious about this unconventional subculture, the Hobo Museum is a fascinating and educational stop that will broaden your horizons.

5. The Future Birthplace of James T. Kirk (Riverside, IA)

Calling all Star Trek fans! Make a pilgrimage to the Future Birthplace of James T. Kirk in Riverside, Iowa. According to Star Trek lore, the legendary Starfleet Captain will be born in this small town on March 22, 2228.

Visit the site of Kirk's future home, marked by a commemorative plaque and a bench where you can sit and ponder the infinite possibilities of space exploration. Take a photo with the life-size statue of Captain Kirk, complete with his iconic Starfleet uniform and phaser.

The town of Riverside fully embraces its claim to fame, hosting an annual Trek-Fest celebration that includes costume contests, trivia games, and a parade. Whether you're a die-hard Trekkie or simply appreciate the power of imagination, the Future Birthplace of James T. Kirk is a quirky and fun stop that will transport you to the final frontier.

6. The World's Largest Bull (Audubon, IA)

Moove over, ordinary roadside attractions! The World's Largest Bull in Audubon is a sight to behold. Standing at 30 feet tall and weighing in at 45 tons, Albert the Bull is a massive concrete and steel sculpture that pays homage to the importance of the cattle industry in Iowa.

Created in 1964 by local artist Jack Kershaw, Albert the Bull has become a beloved landmark and a symbol of the town's agricultural heritage. Visitors can admire the intricate details of the sculpture, from the realistic wrinkles on Albert's face to the texture of his hide.

Take a photo with this gentle giant and learn about the history of cattle farming in Iowa. The World's Largest Bull is a quirky and impressive stop that will leave you in awe of the creativity and ingenuity of small-town America.

7. The Villisca Axe Murder House (Villisca, IA)

Step into a real-life murder mystery at the Villisca Axe Murder House in Villisca. On June 10, 1912, eight people were brutally murdered with an axe in this unassuming Iowa farmhouse, and the case remains unsolved to this day.

Take a guided tour of the house and learn about the chilling details of the crime, the suspects, and the theories surrounding the case. See the original furnishings and artifacts from the time of the murders, and experience the eerie atmosphere that has made the house a popular destination for paranormal investigators.

The Villisca Axe Murder House is a chilling and fascinating stop that will appeal to true crime enthusiasts and history buffs alike. Just be warned: the house is rumored to be haunted, so enter at your own risk!

8. The Buddy Holly Crash Site (Clear Lake, IA)

Pay your respects to a fallen rock and roll legend at the Buddy Holly Crash Site in Clear Lake. On February 3, 1959, Buddy Holly, Ritchie Valens, and J.P. "The Big Bopper" Richardson died in a tragic plane crash near this small Iowa town.

Visit the memorial site, marked by a simple pair of black glasses similar to the ones Holly wore. Read the plaque that honors the lives and music of the three musicians, and reflect on the impact they had on the history of rock and roll.

The crash site is located in a quiet field, surrounded by corn and soybeans, creating a peaceful and contemplative atmosphere. The Buddy Holly Crash Site is a moving and poignant stop that will remind you of the fragility of life and the enduring power of music.

101 Bizarre, Quirky and Totally Fun Adventures in ...

* * *

From the whimsical charm of the World's Largest Wooden Nickel to the chilling mystery of the Villisca Axe Murder House, Iowa's quirky attractions offer a glimpse into the state's rich history, culture, and creativity. These eight adventures are just a small sample of the many hidden gems waiting to be discovered in the Hawkeye State.

Whether you're a curious traveler or a lifelong resident, these bizarre and delightful destinations will leave you with unforgettable memories and a newfound appreciation for Iowa's unique spirit. So, grab your sense of adventure, your camera, and your love for the unconventional, and set out to explore the weird and wonderful side of Iowa. You never know what surprises await you in the heart of the Heartland!

Chapter 5

Kansas: Sunflower State Surprises and Delights

Kansas, known as the Sunflower State, is a land of wide-open prairies, friendly faces, and a rich history that has shaped the American heartland. But beyond the endless fields of wheat and the iconic imagery of "The Wizard of Oz," Kansas is home to a treasure trove of quirky, bizarre, and utterly enchanting adventures waiting to be discovered.

From a museum dedicated to the world's largest collection of salt and pepper shakers to a giant Van Gogh painting on an easel, Kansas is full of surprises that will make you smile and marvel at the creativity and ingenuity of its people. Join us as we uncover eight of the most incredible and unusual hidden gems the Sunflower State

101 Bizarre, Quirky and Totally Fun Adventures in ...

has to offer. Get ready to embrace your inner adventurer and embark on a journey through the delightfully unexpected and endlessly entertaining side of Kansas.

* * *

1. The Evel Knievel Museum (Topeka, KS)

The Evel Knievel Museum, located in Topeka, Kansas, is a must-visit destination for tourists interested in the life and legacy of the legendary stunt performer. Spanning 13,000 square feet across two stories, the museum houses the world's largest collection of authentic Evel Knievel memorabilia. Visitors can explore exhibits arranged in chronological order, showcasing Knievel's life from his early years in Butte, Montana to the height of his fame in the 1970s.

Among the museum's highlights are Knievel's original jump bikes, performance leathers, helmets, and wardrobe, as well as his famous Mack truck, "Big Red." Interactive exhibits, such as the "4D Virtual Reality Jump" featuring Doug Danger, allow visitors to experience the thrill of Knievel's stunts firsthand without the risks. Other notable artifacts include the Snake River Canyon Skycycle-X2, crash helmets from Caesars Palace and Wembley Stadium, and personal effects like family photographs, contracts, and letters.

In addition to the exhibits, the Evel Knievel Museum offers a gift shop, barbecue restaurant, event space, and Yesterday's museum. The museum is open Tuesday through Saturday from 10am to 6pm, with additional hours on Sundays during the summer. Named one of the top 10 best new national attractions in 2017 by USA Today, the Evel Knievel Museum is officially authorized by the Knievel estate and provides a fascinating glimpse into the life of one of America's most iconic daredevils.

2. The Garden of Eden (Lucas, KS)

Step into a world of surreal beauty and eccentric art at the Garden of Eden in Lucas, Kansas. This otherworldly sculpture garden, created by Civil War veteran S.P. Dinsmoor in the early 20th century, features over 150 concrete sculptures depicting biblical scenes, political allegories, and Dinsmoor's own unique vision of the world.

Wander through the lush grounds and marvel at the towering figures, intricate details, and thought-provoking themes of the sculptures. Learn about Dinsmoor's life and the incredible story behind the creation of this one-of-a-kind art environment.

The Garden of Eden is a testament to the power of individual vision and the enduring legacy of outsider art. It's a place that will inspire you to think outside the box and embrace the beauty and strangeness of the world around you.

3. The World's Largest Czech Egg (Wilson, KS)

In the small town of Wilson, Kansas, you'll find a sight that will make you do a double-take. Standing at over 20 feet tall and weighing in at a whopping 2,800 pounds, the World's Largest Czech Egg is a true masterpiece of folk art.

The egg, which is made of fiberglass and painted in a traditional Czech design, was created in 1982 by local artist Mildred Hubka as a tribute to the town's Czech heritage. It's a symbol of the community's pride and a celebration of the rich cultural traditions that have shaped the region. Visitors can take photos with the giant egg, and even explore the nearby Czech Museum, which features exhibits on the history and culture of the Czech people in Kansas. The World's Largest Czech Egg is a whimsical and heartwarming attraction that will leave you with a renewed appreciation for the power of community and tradition.

4. The Kansas Barbed Wire Museum (La Crosse, KS)

Get tangled up in a piece of American history at the Kansas Barbed Wire Museum in La Crosse, Kansas. This unique museum, housed in a restored limestone building from the 1880s, features over 2,000 varieties of barbed wire from around the world.

Learn about the history and evolution of barbed wire, from its early use as a military defense to its role in the settlement of the American West. See rare and unusual examples of barbed wire, including wires with elaborate twists, colorful designs, and even wires made from unusual materials like gold and silver.

The Kansas Barbed Wire Museum is a fascinating and educational destination that will give you a new perspective on this humble but important invention. It's a reminder of the ingenuity and resourcefulness of the pioneers who shaped our nation's history.

5. The World's Largest Easel (Goodland, KS)

Get ready to paint the town red (or any color you like) at the World's Largest Easel in Goodland, Kansas. This towering structure, standing at 80 feet tall and weighing over 40,000 pounds, is a true marvel of engineering and a testament to the power of community spirit.

The easel, which was erected in 2001, holds a giant replica of Vincent van Gogh's famous painting "Three Sunflowers in a Vase". The painting itself measures 24 x 32 feet and was created by local artist Cameron Cross.

Visitors can admire the incredible scale and detail of the painting, and even take a selfie with the giant easel in the background. The World's Largest Easel is a quirky and inspiring attraction that will make you look at art (and the world) in a whole new way.

6. The Grassroots Art Center (Lucas, KS)

Discover the raw talent and unbridled creativity of Kansas's grassroots artists at the Grassroots Art Center in Lucas, Kansas. This unique museum, housed in a restored limestone building from the 1880s, features an eclectic collection of art created by self-taught and outsider artists from across the state.

Marvel at the incredible variety and originality of the artworks, from colorful mosaics and whimsical sculptures to intricate paintings and hand-carved furniture. Learn about the stories and inspirations behind each piece, and gain a new appreciation for the power of art to transform lives and communities.

The Grassroots Art Center is a celebration of the human spirit and the endless possibilities of creative expression. It's a place that will inspire you to unleash your own inner artist and explore the world with fresh eyes and an open heart.

7. The Big Well (Greensburg, KS)

Get ready to drop your jaw (and a penny) at the Big Well in Greensburg, Kansas. This massive hand-dug well, measuring 109 feet deep and 32 feet in diameter, was built in 1887 as a source of water for the bustling railroad town.

Descend the 105 steps to the bottom of the well and marvel at the sheer scale and ingenuity of this incredible feat of engineering. Learn about the history of the well and the town of Greensburg, which was devastated by a massive tornado in 2007 but has since rebuilt itself as a model of sustainable living.

The Big Well is a testament to the resilience and determination of the Kansas spirit. It's a place that will leave you in awe of the power of human perseverance and the enduring beauty of the American heartland.

8. The Kansas Underground Salt Museum (Hutchinson, KS)

Descend into a world of subterranean wonder at the Kansas Underground Salt

Museum in Hutchinson, Kansas. This one-of-a-kind museum, located 650 feet below the Earth's surface in a working salt mine, offers a fascinating glimpse into the history and science of salt mining.

Take a guided tour of the mine and marvel at the incredible underground landscape, complete with towering pillars of salt and shimmering crystal formations. Learn about the process of mining salt and the vital role it plays in our daily lives, from seasoning our food to de-icing our roads.

The Kansas Underground Salt Museum is a unique and unforgettable destination that will leave you with a newfound appreciation for the hidden wonders of the world beneath our feet. It's a place that will remind you of the incredible diversity and complexity of the natural world, and the ingenuity of the humans who have learned to harness its power.

* * *

From the towering easel of Goodland to the subterranean salt mines of Hutchinson, Kansas's quirky attractions offer a glimpse into the state's rich history, vibrant culture, and enduring spirit. These eight adventures

101 Bizarre, Quirky and Totally Fun Adventures in ...

are just a small taste of the many hidden gems waiting to be discovered in the Sunflower State.

Whether you're a lifelong resident or a curious traveler, these surprises and delights will leave you with unforgettable memories and a newfound appreciation for Kansas's unique character. So grab your sense of adventure, your camera, and your love for the unexpected, and set out to explore the weird and wonderful side of Kansas. You never know what amazing discoveries await you in the heart of the heartland!

Chapter 6

Michigan: Great Lakes State Wonders and Oddities

Michigan, affectionately known as the Great Lakes State, is a land of natural beauty, rich history, and a unique blend of quirky and captivating attractions. From the shores of the mighty lakes to the depths of the dense forests, Michigan is a treasure trove of adventures waiting to be discovered.

But beyond the picturesque landscapes and charming small towns lies a world of bizarre, fun, and utterly unforgettable experiences that will leave you in awe. Join us as we embark on a journey through eight of the most incredible and unusual hidden gems the Great Lakes State has to offer. Get ready to embrace your inner explorer and uncover the wonders and oddities that make Michigan truly one-of-a-kind.

101 Bizarre, Quirky and Totally Fun Adventures in ...

* * *

1. The Mystery Spot (St. Ignace, MI)

Step into a world where the laws of gravity seem to bend at The Mystery Spot in St. Ignace, Michigan. This peculiar attraction, located in the heart of the Upper Peninsula, has been baffling visitors since the 1950s with its strange and unexplainable phenomena.

Take a guided tour through the mysterious cabin and marvel at the bizarre optical illusions and gravity-defying stunts. Watch as water flows uphill, people appear to grow and shrink, and balls roll in unexpected directions. Is it a vortex, a magnetic anomaly, or something else entirely? You be the judge!

The Mystery Spot is a classic American roadside attraction that will leave you scratching your head and grinning from ear to ear. It's a place where reality meets illusion, and the impossible becomes possible.

2. The Heidelberg Project (Detroit, MI)

Discover a world of color, creativity, and community at The Heidelberg Project in Detroit, Michigan. This outdoor art installation, spanning two city blocks, is the brainchild of local artist Tyree Guyton, who has transformed abandoned houses and vacant lots into a living canvas of hope and inspiration.

Wander through the vibrant streets and marvel at the incredible array of found-object sculptures, painted polka dots, and whimsical installations. From the famous "Dotty Wotty House" to the "Party Animal House," each artwork tells a story of resilience, joy, and the power of imagination.

The Heidelberg Project is more than just an art museum; it's a testament to the spirit of Detroit and the transformative power of art. It's a place that will inspire you to see beauty in the unexpected and find hope in the face of adversity.

3. The Nun Doll Museum (Indian River, MI)

Get ready to be both charmed and slightly unnerved at The Nun Doll Museum in Indian River, Michigan. This unique collection, housed in a quaint little shop called The Old Habit, features over 500 dolls dressed in traditional nun's habits from around the world.

Marvel at the incredible variety and detail of the dolls, from the classic black and white habits to colorful ethnic attire. Learn about the history and significance of nuns in different cultures and religious orders, and even take home a doll of your own as a one-of-a-kind souvenir.

The Nun Doll Museum is a quirky and fascinating destination that will leave you with a newfound appreciation for the art of doll-making and the enduring legacy of women in religious life. It's a place that will make you smile, ponder, and perhaps even say a little prayer.

4. The Dinosaur Gardens (Ossineke, MI)

Step back in time and walk among the giants at The Dinosaur Gardens in Ossineke, Michigan. This unique outdoor museum, nestled in the woods of Northeast Michigan, features over 25 life-size dinosaur sculptures created by local artist Paul N. Domke in the 1930s.

Wander through the lush forest trails and marvel at the incredible detail and artistry of the sculptures, from the towering T-Rex to the gentle Brontosaurus. Learn about the different dinosaur species and their habits, and even enjoy a picnic in the Prehistoric Forest.

The Dinosaur Gardens is a beloved Michigan landmark that has been delighting visitors of all ages for generations. It's a place that will awaken your inner child and inspire you to dream big and let your imagination run wild.

5. The Pickle Barrel House Museum (Grand Marais, MI)

Get ready to relish in the whimsy and charm of The Pickle Barrel House Museum in Grand Marais, Michigan. This one-of-a-kind structure, built in 1926 by the Pioneer Cooperage Company as a summer cottage, is shaped like a giant wooden pickle barrel and stands two stories tall.

Step inside the cozy interior and marvel at the intricate woodwork, curved walls, and vintage furnishings. Learn about the history of the cooperage industry in Michigan and the clever marketing tactics that led to the creation of this unusual dwelling.

The Pickle Barrel House Museum is a testament to the ingenuity and humor of a bygone era. It's a place that will make you smile, laugh, and appreciate the simple joys of life.

6. The Hamtramck Disneyland (Hamtramck, MI)

Discover a world of whimsy and wonder at The Hamtramck Disneyland in Hamtramck, Michigan. This incredible folk art installation, created by Ukrainian immigrant Dmytro Szylak over the course of 30 years, features a dizzying array of colorful sculptures, kinetic art, and found objects that will leave you in awe.

Wander through the backyard wonderland and marvel at the towering structures made from recycled materials, the spinning windmills, and the twinkling lights. Learn about Szylak's life story and his vision for creating a place of joy and inspiration for his community.

The Hamtramck Disneyland is a hidden gem that celebrates the power of imagination and the beauty of the human spirit. It's a place that will remind you of the magic that can be found in the most unexpected places.

7. The Great Lakes Shipwreck Historical Society (Paradise, MI)

Dive into the haunting history of the Great Lakes at The Great Lakes Shipwreck Historical Society in Paradise, Michigan. This fascinating museum, located at the Whitefish Point Light Station, is dedicated to preserving the memory of the ships and crews lost on the treacherous waters of Lake Superior.

Explore the exhibits and artifacts that tell the stories of famous shipwrecks like the Edmund Fitzgerald, the Daniel J. Morrell, and the Cyprus. Learn about the brave men and women who risked their lives to save others, and the enduring mystery of the ships that vanished without a trace.

The Great Lakes Shipwreck Historical Society is a powerful and moving destination that will give you a newfound respect for the power and beauty of the Great Lakes. It's a place that will remind you of the fragility of life and the enduring human spirit.

8. The Cherry Point Farm and Market (Shelby, MI)

Get lost in a world of sweet delights and agricultural wonders at The Cherry Point Farm and Market in Shelby, Michigan. This charming family-owned farm, located in the heart of Michigan's Fruit Belt, is famous for its delicious cherries, homemade pies, and the world's largest cherry pit spit.

Wander through the lush cherry orchards and sample the juicy fruits straight from the tree. Indulge in a slice of their famous cherry pie, made with a secret family recipe passed down through generations. And don't forget to try your hand at the cherry pit spit, where you can compete against other visitors to see who can spit a cherry pit the farthest!

Travel with Jack and Kitty

The Cherry Point Farm and Market is a wholesome and delightful destination that will give you a taste of the simple pleasures of farm life. It's a place that will remind you of the beauty of nature and the joy of sharing good food with good people.

* * *

From the mind-bending mysteries of The Mystery Spot to the sweet delights of The Cherry Point Farm and Market, Michigan's quirky attractions offer a glimpse into the state's rich history, vibrant culture, and enduring spirit. These eight adventures are just a small taste of the many hidden gems waiting to be discovered in the Great Lakes State.

Whether you're a lifelong resident or a curious traveler, these wonders and oddities will leave you with unforgettable memories and a newfound appreciation for Michigan's unique character. So grab your sense of adventure, your camera, and your love for the unexpected, and set out to explore the weird and wonderful side of Michigan. You never know what amazing discoveries await you in the heart of the Great Lakes!

Chapter 7

Minnesota: Land of 10,000 Wacky Adventures

Minnesota, the Land of 10,000 Lakes, is also home to a plethora of quirky, bizarre, and totally fun adventures waiting to be discovered. From giant statues and unique museums to outdoor sculptures and underground mines, the North Star State offers a treasure trove of hidden gems that will delight and surprise visitors of all ages.

Join us as we explore 13 of the most amazing and unusual attractions Minnesota has to offer, each with its own fascinating story and charm. Get ready to step off the beaten path and into a world of wonder, laughter, and unforgettable memories.

* * *

1. The SPAM Museum (Austin, MN)

Embrace your inner foodie and visit the SPAM Museum, celebrating the iconic canned meat that has fed generations. Learn about the history of SPAM, from its humble beginnings during the Great Depression to its role in feeding troops during World War II. Discover how this simple meat product became a global phenomenon and a beloved part of American culture.

Try your hand at canning your own SPAM in the interactive exhibit, and even sample some creative SPAM recipes, such as SPAM musubi and SPAM sliders. The museum also features a variety of SPAM-themed memorabilia, including vintage advertisements, cookbooks, and collectibles.

Don't forget to snap a photo with the giant SPAM can outside the museum, a perfect backdrop for your social media feed. The SPAM Museum is a quirky and delightful attraction that celebrates the enduring legacy of this iconic American brand.

101 Bizarre, Quirky and Totally Fun Adventures in ...

2. The Jolly Green Giant Statue (Blue Earth, MN)

Stand in awe before the 55-foot-tall Jolly Green Giant statue, a tribute to the beloved vegetable mascot. The statue, built in 1979, welcomes visitors to the city of Blue Earth and serves as a symbol of the region's agricultural heritage.

Take a selfie with the towering giant, whose friendly smile and outstretched hand make for a perfect photo opportunity. Explore the visitor center nearby to learn about the history of the Green Giant company, which began as the Minnesota Valley Canning Company in 1903.

Discover how the company grew from a small local business to a global brand, thanks in part to the success of its mascot, the Jolly Green Giant. The statue and visitor center offer a fun and educational experience that celebrates the importance of agriculture in the heartland of America.

3. The World's Largest Ball of Twine (Darwin, MN)

Marvel at the world's largest ball of twine, created by one man, Francis A. Johnson, over the course of 29 years. Johnson began winding the twine in 1950 as a hobby, and continued adding to it until his death in 1989.

The ball weighs over 17,000 pounds and measures 12 feet in diameter, making it a true marvel of dedication and perseverance. Visitors can walk around the ball and even touch it, feeling the intricate winding of the twine that Johnson completed by hand.

The World's Largest Ball of Twine is a testament to the power of a simple idea and the determination of one man to see it through. It's a quirky and fascinating attraction that celebrates the unique spirit of small-town America.

4. The Bakken Museum (Minneapolis, MN)

Discover the electrifying world of science and technology at The Bakken Museum. Explore the fascinating history of electricity and its impact on medicine through interactive exhibits and demonstrations. Get hands-on with vintage medical devices, such as early X-ray machines and electrotherapy instruments, and learn about the pioneers who harnessed the power of electricity to revolutionize healthcare.

Witness captivating electrical phenomena in the Frankenstein's Laboratory exhibit, which brings to life the science behind Mary Shelley's classic novel. See the sparks fly from a giant Tesla coil, and learn about the ethical questions surrounding the use of electricity in medicine.

The museum is housed in a beautiful historic mansion on the shores of Lake Calhoun, adding to its unique charm. Stroll through the picturesque gardens and enjoy the serene lakeside setting after your mind-boggling journey through the world of electricity and medicine. The Bakken Museum is a hidden gem that combines science, history, and a dash of quirkiness, making it a must-visit destination for curious minds of all ages.

5. The Largest Free-Standing Hockey Stick (Eveleth, MN)

Pay homage to Minnesota's hockey heritage at the Largest Free-Standing Hockey Stick. This massive stick measures 110 feet long and weighs over 10,000 pounds, making it a true feat of engineering and a testament to the state's love for the sport.

The stick was created in 1995 as part of the "Stick Project," a community effort to celebrate Eveleth's hockey history and attract visitors to the small town. The project was a success, and the stick has become an iconic landmark and a popular spot for photos.

Take a moment to appreciate the craftsmanship and dedication that went into creating this enormous stick, which is made of steel and fiberglass. Learn about the history of hockey in Minnesota, from the early days of pond hockey to the state's numerous Olympic and NHL players. The Largest Free-Standing Hockey Stick is a must-see attraction for hockey fans and anyone who appreciates the unique culture and spirit of the North Star State.

6. The Judy Garland Museum (Grand Rapids, MN)

Follow the yellow brick road to the Judy Garland Museum, dedicated to the life and career of the legendary actress. Born in Grand Rapids in 1922, Garland rose to fame as a child star and went on to become one of the most beloved entertainers of the 20th century.

See rare photographs, costumes, and memorabilia from Garland's iconic role as Dorothy in "The Wizard of Oz," including the original carriage used in the film. Explore exhibits that showcase Garland's personal life, including her childhood home and her struggles with addiction and mental health.

Don't miss the chance to see the world's largest Judy Garland collection, which includes over 3,000 items related to the actress's life and career. The museum also hosts special events throughout the year, including the annual Judy Garland Festival in June. Whether you're a die-hard fan or simply appreciate the magic of classic Hollywood, the Judy Garland Museum is a fascinating and moving tribute to one of America's greatest talents.

7. The LARK Toys Store (Kellogg), MN

Unleash your inner child at the LARK Toys Store, featuring a hand-carved carousel, a massive selection of toys, and an impressive collection of marbles. Step into a world of wonder and imagination as you explore the store's 20,000 square feet of playtime paradise.

Take a ride on the beautifully crafted carousel, which features 24 hand-carved and painted animals, including a majestic unicorn and a friendly dragon. Browse the store's extensive collection of toys, from classic wooden blocks and puzzles to the latest high-tech gadgets.

Marvel at the intricate marble sculptures and the store's collection of over 1,000 marbles, some of which date back to the 1800s. LARK Toys also features a mini-golf course, a cafe, and a toy museum, making it a perfect destination for a day of family fun. Whether you're young or simply young at heart, the LARK Toys Store is a whimsical and delightful adventure that will leave you smiling.

8. The Franconia Sculpture Park (Franconia, MN)

Discover a hidden gem at the Franconia Sculpture Park, showcasing over 120 stunning sculptures created by artists from around the world. Set on 43 acres of scenic countryside, the park is a unique blend of art and nature that invites visitors to explore and engage with the landscape.

Wander through the park's winding trails, discovering diverse and thought-provoking artworks that range from towering metal structures to delicate glass installations. Many of the sculptures are interactive, encouraging visitors to touch, climb, and even play with the art.

The park also offers a variety of educational programs and events throughout the year, including artist talks, workshops, and live performances. Whether you're an art enthusiast or simply appreciate the beauty of the outdoors, the Franconia Sculpture Park is a must-visit destination that will inspire and delight you.

9. The Minneapolis Sculpture Garden (Minneapolis, MN)

Explore the iconic Minneapolis Sculpture Garden, home to the famous "Spoonbridge and Cherry" sculpture. This whimsical and beloved artwork, created by Claes Oldenburg and Coosje van Bruggen, has become a symbol of the city and a favorite spot for photos.

Stroll through the 11-acre park, discovering more than 40 unique sculptures and installations by renowned artists such as Henry Moore, Frank Gehry, and Jenny Holzer. The garden's diverse collection includes abstract and figurative works, as well as interactive pieces that invite visitors to explore and play.

The Minneapolis Sculpture Garden is a perfect spot for a picnic or a leisurely afternoon of art appreciation. The park also hosts special events throughout the year, including live music performances and outdoor movie screenings. With its stunning artworks and beautiful natural setting, the Minneapolis Sculpture Garden is a must-see attraction for anyone visiting the Twin Cities.

10. The House of Balls (Minneapolis, MN)

Step into the quirky world of the House of Balls, a unique art gallery and studio featuring thousands of balls in various sizes and materials. Created by eccentric artist Allen Christian, the House of Balls is a one-of-a-kind experience that will leave you amazed and amused.

Explore the gallery's eclectic collection of ball-themed artworks, from giant wooden spheres to intricate metal sculptures. Learn about Christian's creative process and his fascination with the shape and symbolism of the ball.

The House of Balls also offers visitors the chance to create their own ball-themed artwork in the studio's workshops. Try your hand at welding, woodworking, or painting, and take home a unique souvenir of your visit. Whether you're an art lover or simply appreciate the unconventional, the House of Balls is a must-visit destination that celebrates the power of creativity and imagination.

11. The Tapemark Charity Pro-Am Golf Tournament (West St. Paul, MN)

Witness the wackiest golf tournament in the Midwest at the Tapemark Charity Pro-Am. This annual event brings together professional and amateur golfers for a day of hilarious and entertaining competition, all in the name of raising money for a good cause.

Watch as players compete in outrageous costumes, using unconventional golf clubs and navigating through zany obstacles. From oversized clown shoes to hockey sticks and even a rubber chicken, the golfers use their creativity and humor to conquer the course and entertain the crowds.

The tournament raises funds for local charities that support individuals with developmental disabilities, making it a fun and meaningful event for everyone involved. Whether you're a golf enthusiast or simply appreciate a good laugh, the Tapemark Charity Pro-Am is a must-see event that combines sport, comedy, and community spirit.

12. The Soudan Underground Mine State Park (Soudan, MN)

Descend into the depths of the Earth at the Soudan Underground Mine State Park. This former iron ore mine, which operated from 1882 to 1962, offers visitors a unique and fascinating glimpse into the history of mining in Minnesota.

Take a guided tour of the mine, riding the rickety elevator down 2,341 feet to the 27th level. Explore the underground tunnels and caverns, learning about the tools and techniques used by the miners who worked in the dark, damp, and dangerous conditions.

See the impressive machinery and equipment that was used to extract the iron ore, including the massive hoist that lifted the ore to the surface. Learn about the hardships faced by the miners, from the constant threat of cave-ins to the health risks associated with breathing in the mine's dust and fumes. The Soudan Underground Mine State Park is a powerful and educational experience that offers a rare look into the hard work and sacrifice that built America's industry.

13. The Pavek Museum of Broadcasting (St. Louis Park, MN)

Step back in time at the Pavek Museum of Broadcasting, showcasing the history of radio and television. Explore the museum's extensive collection of vintage radio equipment, television sets, and memorabilia from the golden age of broadcasting.

See the evolution of radio technology, from the early crystal sets of the 1920s to the sleek designs of the 1950s. Learn about the pioneers who shaped the industry, including Minnesota's own Earl Bakken, who invented the first transistorized pacemaker. Discover the impact of broadcasting on American culture, from the live radio shows of the 1930s to the rise of television in the 1950s and beyond. The Pavek Museum also offers a variety of interactive exhibits and educational programs, allowing visitors to experience the magic of broadcasting firsthand. Whether you're a history buff or a media enthusiast, the Pavek Museum of Broadcasting is a fascinating and nostalgic journey through the airwaves of the past.

* * *

From the whimsical charm of the SPAM Museum to the awe-inspiring depths of the Soudan Underground Mine, Minnesota's quirky attractions offer a glimpse into the state's rich history, culture, and creativity. These 13 adventures are just a small sample of the many hidden gems waiting to be discovered in the Land of 10,000 Lakes.

So pack your bags, grab your sense of humor, and get ready to embark on a journey through the weird, wonderful, and totally fun side of Minnesota. Whether

101 Bizarre, Quirky and Totally Fun Adventures in ...

you're a lifelong resident or a first-time visitor, these bizarre and delightful attractions will leave you with a newfound appreciation for the North Star State's unique spirit and charm.

Chapter 8

Missouri: Show-Me State Marvels and Curiosities

Missouri, the Show-Me State, is a land of natural beauty, rich history, and a delightful array of quirky and captivating attractions. From the rolling hills of the Ozarks to the bustling streets of St. Louis and Kansas City, Missouri is filled with hidden gems waiting to be uncovered. But beyond the well-known landmarks and tourist hotspots lies a world of bizarre, fun, and utterly unforgettable experiences that will leave you amazed and amused.

Join us as we embark on a journey through eight of the most incredible and unusual adventures the Show-Me State has to offer. Get ready to embrace your inner explorer and discover the marvels and curiosities that make Missouri truly one-of-a-kind.

* * *

1. The World's Largest Chess Piece (St. Louis, MO)

Make your move and marvel at The World's Largest Chess Piece in St. Louis, Missouri. This colossal king piece, standing at an impressive 14 feet tall and weighing over 2,000 pounds, is a testament to the city's love for the game of chess.

Located outside the World Chess Hall of Fame, this massive sculpture was created by artist Aidan Demarco and unveiled in 2018. The piece is made of stainless steel and features intricate details that showcase the beauty and complexity of the game.

Take a photo with this larger-than-life king and explore the nearby World Chess Hall of Fame, which features exhibits on the history and culture of chess from around the world. Whether you're a seasoned grandmaster or a casual player, The World's Largest Chess Piece is a must-see attraction that will leave you in awe of the power and elegance of the game.

2. The Glore Psychiatric Museum (St. Joseph, MO)

Step into the haunting and fascinating world of mental health treatment at The Glore Psychiatric Museum in St. Joseph, Missouri. This unique museum, located in a former state psychiatric hospital, offers a rare glimpse into the history of mental health care and the lives of those who lived and worked within its walls.

Explore the exhibits and artifacts that showcase the evolution of psychiatric treatment, from the barbaric practices of the past to the more humane approaches of the present. See the original patient artwork, medical equipment, and personal belongings that tell the stories of those who suffered from mental illness and the caregivers who sought to help them.

The Glore Psychiatric Museum is a powerful and thought-provoking destination that will challenge your perceptions and deepen your understanding of mental health. It's a place that will remind you of the resilience of the human spirit and the importance of compassion and empathy in the face of suffering.

3. The Jesse James Wax Museum (Stanton, MO)

Relive the thrilling and notorious life of America's most famous outlaw at The Jesse James Wax Museum in Stanton, Missouri. This one-of-a-kind attraction, located in the heart of the Missouri Ozarks, features over 20 life-size wax figures that depict the key moments and characters in the story of Jesse James.

Step into the meticulously recreated scenes and marvel at the incredible detail and artistry of the figures, from the young Jesse and his brother Frank to the infamous Pinkerton detectives who pursued them. Learn about the real history behind the legend and separate fact from fiction in the museum's informative exhibits.

The Jesse James Wax Museum is a fun and fascinating destination that will transport you back to the Wild West and the golden age of the American outlaw. It's a place that will inspire your imagination and leave you with a newfound appreciation for the enduring power of a good story.

4. The Precious Moments Chapel (Carthage, MO)

Discover a world of innocence, love, and inspiration at The Precious Moments Chapel in Carthage, Missouri. This stunning chapel, built in 1989 by artist Samuel J. Butcher, is a tribute to the beloved Precious Moments figurines and the messages of faith, hope, and love they represent.

Step inside the chapel and marvel at the breathtaking murals, stained glass windows, and hand-painted ceiling that tell the story of God's love for humanity. See the original Precious Moments figurines that inspired the artwork and learn about the life and vision of their creator.

The Precious Moments Chapel is a peaceful and uplifting destination that will touch your heart and renew your spirit. It's a place that will remind you of the beauty and power of simple acts of kindness and the importance of cherishing the precious moments in life.

5. The Nuclear Waste Adventure Trail (Weldon Spring, MO)

Embark on a one-of-a-kind journey through the history of the nuclear age at The Nuclear Waste Adventure Trail in Weldon Spring, Missouri. This unique hiking trail, located on the site of a former uranium processing plant, offers a fascinating glimpse into the complex and controversial history of nuclear energy and waste management.

Follow the trail markers and informative signs that guide you through the site, from the massive 75-foot-tall disposal cell that holds the contaminated waste to the restored native prairie that now thrives in its place. Learn about the science and technology behind nuclear energy, the environmental and health impacts of nuclear waste, and the ongoing efforts to clean up and protect the site.

The Nuclear Waste Adventure Trail is a thought-provoking and educational destination that will challenge your assumptions and broaden your understanding of one of the most important issues of our time. It's a place that will remind you of the power and responsibility of science and the importance of preserving our natural world for future generations.

6. Leila's Hair Museum (Independence, MO)

Get ready to let your hair down and marvel at the wonders of Leila's Hair Museum in Independence, Missouri. This quirky and fascinating museum, the only one of its kind in the world, features over 600 wreaths and over 2,000 pieces of jewelry made from human hair dating back to the 17th century.

Explore the intricate and beautiful designs created by skilled artisans using the hair of loved ones as a symbol of devotion, mourning, and remembrance. Learn about the history and cultural significance of hairwork and the stories behind the pieces on display.

Leila's Hair Museum is a unique and captivating destination that will challenge your notions of art and beauty and leave you with a newfound appreciation for the creativity and skill of our ancestors. It's a place that will make you look at hair in a whole new way and remind you of the enduring power of love and memory.

7. The Vacuum Cleaner Museum (St. James, MO)

Prepare to be swept away by the fascinating and quirky world of vacuum cleaners at The Vacuum Cleaner Museum in St. James, Missouri. This one-of-a-kind museum, located in the heart of the Missouri Ozarks, features over 500 vintage and modern vacuum cleaners from around the world.

Marvel at the incredible variety and ingenuity of the designs, from the earliest manual models to the high-tech robotic vacuums of today. Learn about the history and evolution of the vacuum cleaner and its impact on domestic life and popular culture.

The Vacuum Cleaner Museum is a fun and educational destination that will appeal to anyone with a love for gadgets, history, or just plain quirkiness. It's a place that will make you appreciate the humble household appliance in a whole new light and remind you of the power of human innovation and creativity.

8. The Devil's Icebox (Rocheport, MO)

Descend into the depths of the Earth and explore the chilling wonders of The Devil's Icebox in Rocheport, Missouri. This massive cave system, located in Rock Bridge Memorial State Park, features over 7 miles of mapped passages and a unique underground stream that flows through the caverns.

Embark on a guided tour and marvel at the stunning rock formations, from the towering stalactites to the delicate soda straws. Learn about the geology and ecology of the cave and the diverse array of wildlife that calls it home, including several species of bats and the rare grotto salamander.

The Devil's Icebox is a thrilling and unforgettable destination that will awaken your sense of adventure and leave you in awe of the hidden wonders of the natural world. It's a place that will remind you of the power and beauty of the underground realm and the importance of preserving these fragile ecosystems for generations to come.

* * *

101 Bizarre, Quirky and Totally Fun Adventures in ...

From the awe-inspiring heights of The World's Largest Chess Piece to the chilling depths of The Devil's Icebox, Missouri's quirky attractions offer a glimpse into the state's rich history, diverse culture, and enduring sense of wonder. These eight adventures are just a small taste of the many hidden gems waiting to be discovered in the Show-Me State.

Whether you're a lifelong resident or a curious traveler, these marvels and curiosities will leave you with unforgettable memories and a newfound appreciation for Missouri's unique character. So grab your sense of adventure, your camera, and your love for the unexpected, and set out to explore the weird and wonderful side of Missouri. You never know what amazing discoveries await you in the heart of the Midwest!

Chapter 9

Nebraska: Cornhusker State Curiosities and Delights

Nebraska, the Cornhusker State, is a land of wide-open prairies, friendly faces, and a surprising array of quirky and captivating attractions. From the towering bluffs of the Panhandle to the rolling hills of the Sandhills, Nebraska is filled with hidden gems waiting to be uncovered.

But beyond the well-known landmarks and tourist hotspots lies a world of bizarre, fun, and utterly unforgettable experiences that will leave you amazed and amused. Join us as we embark on a journey through eight of the most incredible and unusual adventures the Cornhusker State has to offer. Get ready to embrace your inner explorer and discover the curiosities and de-

101 Bizarre, Quirky and Totally Fun Adventures in ...

lights that make Nebraska truly one-of-a-kind.

* * *

1. Carhenge (Alliance, NE)

Step into a world of automotive wonder at Carhenge in Alliance, Nebraska. This unique sculpture park, inspired by the ancient Stonehenge monument in England, features 39 vintage American cars painted gray and arranged in a circular formation that mimics the original stone circle.

Created by artist Jim Reinders in 1987 as a memorial to his father, Carhenge has become a beloved roadside attraction and a testament to the creativity and ingenuity of the American spirit. Walk among the towering cars and marvel at the intricate details and clever positioning that make this sculpture truly one-of-a-kind.

Carhenge is a must-see destination for anyone with a love for art, cars, or just plain quirkiness. It's a place that will make you smile, ponder, and appreciate the power of imagination and the enduring legacy of the American automobile.

2. National Museum of Roller Skating (Lincoln, NE)

The National Museum of Roller Skating, established in 1980, is the only museum of its kind in the world. Celebrating its 40th anniversary in 2020, the museum is dedicated to providing visitors with a unique and enriching experience, showcasing the vibrant history of roller skating through intriguing exhibits and one-of-a-kind artifacts.

Visitors can explore the largest collection of roller skating artifacts and textual materials in the world, including skates, costumes, films, artwork, and other memorabilia dating back to 1819. The museum offers a fascinating journey through the history and development of roller sports and technology, highlighting the shared experience of roller skating as a recreational activity, sport, and business.

The museum is open Monday through Friday, 9am-5pm, and is closed on holidays. Admission is free, making it an accessible and educational experience for all. Located in a historic building formerly used by the Lincoln Telegram and Telegraph Company, the National Museum of Roller Skating shares its space with USA Roller

Sports, the national governing body of roller sports.

3. The World's Largest Ball of Stamps (Boys Town, NE)

In Boys Town, Nebraska, a unique attraction awaits curious visitors: the World's Largest Ball of Stamps. This giant sphere, measuring 32 inches in diameter and weighing approximately 600 pounds, is estimated to contain over four million canceled stamps. The ball is displayed in front of a stunning framed sunburst mural, also made entirely of stamps, creating a captivating sight for stamp collectors and tourists alike.

The origins of this quirky creation date back to 1953 when the Boys Town Stamp Collecting Club began consolidating less-valuable stamps using a golf ball as a base. Although the exact motivation behind the project remains unclear, Mary Haurd, manager of the Boys Town Visitor Center, suspects that the stamp collectors were simply bored. The stamp ball grew steadily until 1955, when it gained national attention after being featured in the syndicated newspaper column, Ripley's Believe It or Not.

Visitors interested in seeing the World's Largest Ball of Stamps can find it on the west side of Boys Town. To reach the attraction, take the US Hwy 6/Dodge St. exit at 137th St., drive south into Boys Town, and take the first left on Flanagan Blvd. The stamp ball is housed in the Leon Myers Stamp Center, which is part of the Boys Town Visitors Center. While admiring the giant sticky sphere, remember to refrain from peeling off any of the stamps.

4. The Cowboy Trail (Valentine, NE)

Saddle up and hit the trail on The Cowboy Trail, the longest rail-to-trail conversion in the United States. Stretching over 195 miles from Valentine to Norfolk, this former Chicago and Northwestern Railway corridor offers a unique and unforgettable way to experience the beauty and history of the Nebraska countryside.

Traverse the stunning sandstone canyons of the Niobrara River Valley, the rolling grasslands of the Sandhills, and the lush farmlands of the Elkhorn River Valley.

101 Bizarre, Quirky and Totally Fun Adventures in ...

Stop at the many small towns and communities along the way to explore their unique history and culture, from the Indigenous heritage of the Ponca and Santee Sioux to the early pioneers and cowboys who settled the region.

The Cowboy Trail is a must-do adventure for anyone with a love for the great outdoors, history, or just plain fun. It's a place that will challenge your endurance, awaken your sense of wonder, and leave you with a newfound appreciation for the rugged beauty and resilient spirit of the American West.

5. The Klown Doll Museum (Plainview, NE)

Step into a world of colorful chaos at The Klown Doll Museum in Plainview, Nebraska. This one-of-a-kind collection, housed in a former children's library, features over 7,000 clown dolls and related items from around the world.

Marvel at the incredible variety and creativity of the dolls, from the classic red-nosed clowns to the more unusual and exotic designs. Learn about the history and cultural significance of clowns and the stories behind the museum's most prized possessions.

The Klown Doll Museum is a fascinating and fun destination that will appeal to anyone with a love for dolls, clowns, or just plain quirkiness. It's a place that will make you laugh, wonder, and maybe even a little bit creeped out, but in the best possible way.

6. The World's Largest Time Capsule (Seward, NE)

Take a trip through time at The World's Largest Time Capsule in Seward, Nebraska. This massive concrete vault, measuring 20 feet long and 8 feet in diameter, was sealed in 1975 during the city's centennial celebration and is scheduled to be opened in 2025, during Seward's sesquicentennial.

Peer through the viewing window and catch a glimpse of the over 5,000 items inside, including books, photographs, clothing, and other artifacts that capture the essence of life in Seward in the 1970s. Learn about the history of time capsules and the significance of this unique project for the community.

101 Bizarre, Quirky and Totally Fun Adventures in ...

The World's Largest Time Capsule is a fascinating and thought-provoking destination that will appeal to anyone with a love for history, science, or just plain curiosity. It's a place that will make you ponder the passage of time, the enduring legacy of human civilization, and the incredible things we can achieve when we work together towards a common goal.

7. The Spinning Yellow Giant (Omaha, NE)

Get ready to go for a spin at The Spinning Yellow Giant in Omaha, Nebraska. This 50-foot-tall, bright yellow sculpture, located in the heart of downtown Omaha, is the world's largest working yo-yo.

Watch in amazement as the massive yo-yo, which weighs over 10,000 pounds, is hoisted up and down by a crane, spinning and twirling in the wind. Learn about the history and science behind the yo-yo and the incredible engineering feat that went into creating this one-of-a-kind attraction.

The Spinning Yellow Giant is a must-see destination for anyone with a love for toys, physics, or just plain fun. It's a place that will make you smile, marvel, and remember the simple joys of childhood and the incredible things that can be achieved with a little bit of creativity and a whole lot of determination.

8. The Petrified Wood Gallery (Ogallala, NE)

Step back in time and discover the ancient wonders of The Petrified Wood Gallery in Ogallala, Nebraska. This unique museum and gift shop features the world's largest collection of petrified wood art, with over 100,000 pieces on display.

Marvel at the incredible colors, patterns, and textures of the petrified wood, which has been transformed over millions of years from living trees into solid stone. Learn about the process of petrification and the fascinating geology of the region, which was once covered by a vast inland sea.

The Petrified Wood Gallery is a must-see destination for anyone with a love for nature, art, or just plain beauty. It's a place that will awaken your sense of wonder, challenge your perception of time and change, and leave you with a newfound appreciation for the incredible diversity and resilience of the natural world.

101 Bizarre, Quirky and Totally Fun Adventures in ...

* * *

From the towering cars of Carhenge to the ancient wonders of The Petrified Wood Gallery, Nebraska's quirky attractions offer a glimpse into the state's rich history, diverse culture, and enduring sense of wonder. These eight adventures are just a small taste of the many hidden gems waiting to be discovered in the Cornhusker State. Whether you're a lifelong resident or a curious traveler, these curiosities and delights will leave you with unforgettable memories and a newfound appreciation for Nebraska's unique character.

So grab your sense of adventure, your camera, and your love for the unexpected, and set out to explore the weird and wonderful side of Nebraska. You never know what amazing discoveries await you in the heart of the Great Plains!

Chapter 10

North Dakota: Roughrider State Oddities and Adventures

North Dakota, known as the Roughrider State, is a land of rugged beauty, rich history, and a surprising array of quirky and captivating attractions. From the badlands of the west to the rolling prairies of the east, North Dakota is filled with hidden gems waiting to be discovered. But beyond the well-known landmarks and tourist hotspots lies a world of bizarre, fun, and utterly unforgettable experiences that will leave you amazed and amused.

Join us as we embark on a journey through eight of the most incredible and unusual adventures the Roughrider State has to offer. Get ready to embrace your inner explorer and uncover the oddities and

101 Bizarre, Quirky and Totally Fun Adventures in ...

adventures that make North Dakota truly one-of-a-kind.

* * *

1. The Enchanted Highway (Regent, ND)

Embark on a magical journey down The Enchanted Highway, a 32-mile stretch of road between Regent and Gladstone, North Dakota. This unique open-air art gallery features seven giant metal sculptures created by local artist Gary Greff, each depicting a different aspect of North Dakota life and culture.

Marvel at the towering "Geese in Flight," the world's largest metal sculpture at 110 feet tall and 154 feet wide. Stop at the "Deer Crossing," where a giant buck and doe appear to leap across the road. Learn about the history and inspiration behind each sculpture and the incredible effort that went into creating these massive works of art.

The Enchanted Highway is a must-see destination for anyone with a love for art, nature, or just plain quirkiness. It's a place that will make you smile, wonder, and appreciate the incredible creativity and dedication of the human spirit.

2. The Dakota Dinosaur Museum (Dickinson, ND)

Step back in time and discover the ancient wonders of The Dakota Dinosaur Museum in Dickinson, North Dakota. This fascinating museum features a wide array of dinosaur fossils, casts, and exhibits that showcase the incredible diversity and history of these prehistoric giants.

Marvel at the towering T-Rex skeleton, the triceratops skull, and the incredibly well-preserved hadrosaur mummy. Learn about the geology and paleontology of the region, which was once part of the vast inland sea that covered much of North America during the Cretaceous period.

The Dakota Dinosaur Museum is a must-see destination for anyone with a love for science, history, or just plain wonder. It's a place that will awaken your inner child, challenge your understanding of the world, and leave you with a newfound appreciation for the incredible mysteries of the past.

3. The Bagg Bonanza Farm (Mooreton, ND)

Experience life on the frontier at The Bagg Bonanza Farm in Mooreton, North Dakota. This living history museum, located on the site of a historic bonanza farm, offers visitors a unique glimpse into the daily life and work of the early settlers who transformed the prairies into a thriving agricultural landscape.

Step inside the beautifully restored farm buildings, including the main house, the bunkhouse, and the blacksmith shop. Watch demonstrations of traditional crafts and skills, such as butter churning, sheep shearing, and horseshoeing. Learn about the incredible hardships and triumphs of the bonanza farmers and the crucial role they played in the development of the Great Plains.

The Bagg Bonanza Farm is a must-see destination for anyone with a love for history, agriculture, or just plain fun. It's a place that will transport you back in time, awaken your sense of wonder, and leave you with a newfound appreciation for the incredible resilience and ingenuity of the human spirit.

4. The World's Largest Buffalo (Jamestown, ND)

Get ready to say "hello" to the World's Largest Buffalo in Jamestown, North Dakota. This massive concrete sculpture, measuring 26 feet tall and 46 feet long, has been a beloved roadside attraction and symbol of the city since its creation in 1959.

Take a selfie with the giant buffalo, affectionately known as "Dakota Thunder," and learn about the history and significance of the American bison in the culture and ecology of the Great Plains. Visit the adjacent National Buffalo Museum to see live bison and learn even more about these majestic creatures.

The World's Largest Buffalo is a must-see destination for anyone with a love for animals, history, or just plain quirkiness. It's a place that will make you smile, marvel, and appreciate the incredible beauty and power of the natural world.

5. The Pyramid of North Dakota (Nekoma, ND)

Discover a piece of Cold War history at The Pyramid of North Dakota in Nekoma. This unique structure, officially known as the Stanley R. Mickelsen Safeguard Complex, was built in the 1970s as part of a missile defense system designed to protect the United States from Soviet nuclear attacks.

Explore the massive concrete pyramid, which housed the radar and computer systems that controlled the missiles. Learn about the history and technology of the Cold War and the incredible engineering feat that went into building this one-of-a-kind structure.

The Pyramid of North Dakota is a must-see destination for anyone with a love for history, science, or just plain curiosity. It's a place that will challenge your understanding of the world, awaken your sense of wonder, and leave you with a newfound appreciation for the incredible complexity and fragility of human civilization.

6. The Scandinavian Heritage Park (Minot, ND)

Celebrate the rich cultural heritage of North Dakota's Scandinavian immigrants at The Scandinavian Heritage Park in Minot. This beautiful 14-acre park features a variety of traditional Scandinavian buildings, sculptures, and exhibits that showcase the history and traditions of the region's Norwegian, Swedish, Danish, Finnish, and Icelandic communities.

Step inside the stunning Gol Stave Church, a full-scale replica of a 12th-century Norwegian church. Marvel at the intricate woodcarvings and colorful rosemaling of the Dala Horse. Learn about the incredible journey and contributions of the Scandinavian immigrants who helped shape the culture and character of North Dakota.

The Scandinavian Heritage Park is a must-see destination for anyone with a love for history, art, or just plain beauty. It's a place that will transport you to another world, awaken your sense of wonder, and leave you with a newfound appreciation for the incredible diversity and richness of human culture.

7. The Welk Homestead State Historic Site (Strasburg, ND)

Take a trip down memory lane at The Welk Homestead State Historic Site in Strasburg, North Dakota. This charming farmstead, located on the site of the childhood home of famous bandleader Lawrence Welk, offers visitors a unique glimpse into the early life and influences of one of America's most beloved entertainers.

Step inside the beautifully restored farmhouse and outbuildings, filled with original family furnishings and memorabilia. Learn about the incredible story of Welk's rise from humble beginnings on the North Dakota prairie to international stardom as the host of the long-running TV show "The Lawrence Welk Show."

The Welk Homestead State Historic Site is a must-see destination for anyone with a love for music, history, or just plain nostalgia. It's a place that will transport you back in time, awaken your sense of joy and wonder, and leave you with a newfound appreciation for the incredible power of the American dream.

8. The Paul Broste Rock Museum (Parshall, ND)

Discover a hidden gem of North Dakota's natural history at The Paul Broste Rock Museum in Parshall. This fascinating museum, housed in a beautiful historic stone building, features an incredible collection of rocks, minerals, and fossils from around the world, collected by local farmer and rock enthusiast Paul Broste over his lifetime.

Marvel at the colorful crystals, geodes, and petrified wood, and learn about the incredible geology and natural history of North Dakota and beyond. Step outside to explore the beautiful landscaped gardens and nature trails, filled with native plants and wildlife.

The Paul Broste Rock Museum is a must-see destination for anyone with a love for nature, science, or just plain beauty. It's a place that will awaken your sense of wonder, challenge your understanding of the world, and leave you with a newfound appreciation for the incredible diversity and complexity of the natural world.

* * *

101 Bizarre, Quirky and Totally Fun Adventures in ...

From the giant sculptures of the Enchanted Highway to the hidden gems of The Paul Broste Rock Museum, North Dakota's quirky attractions offer a glimpse into the state's rich history, diverse culture, and rugged natural beauty. These eight adventures are just a small taste of the many oddities and adventures waiting to be discovered in the Roughrider State.

Whether you're a lifelong resident or a curious traveler, these unique experiences will leave you with unforgettable memories and a newfound appreciation for North Dakota's one-of-a-kind character. So grab your sense of adventure, your camera, and your love for the unexpected, and set out to explore the weird and wonderful side of North Dakota. You never know what amazing discoveries await you in the heart of the Great Plains!

Chapter 11

Ohio: Buckeye State Oddities and Amusements

Ohio, affectionately known as the Buckeye State, is a land of diverse landscapes, rich history, and a delightful array of quirky and captivating attractions. From the shores of Lake Erie to the rolling hills of the Appalachian foothills, Ohio is filled with hidden gems waiting to be discovered. But beyond the well-known landmarks and tourist hotspots lies a world of bizarre, fun, and utterly unforgettable experiences that will leave you amazed and amused.

Join us as we embark on a journey through eight of the most incredible and unusual adventures the Buckeye State has to offer. Get ready to embrace your inner explorer and uncover the oddities and

101 Bizarre, Quirky and Totally Fun Adventures in ...

amusements that make Ohio truly one-of-a-kind.

* * *

1. The Troll Hole Museum (Alliance, OH)

Step into a world of whimsy and wonder at The Troll Hole Museum in Alliance, Ohio. This unique museum, housed in a beautifully restored historic building, boasts the world's largest collection of troll dolls, with over 20,000 of these colorful, wild-haired creatures on display.

Marvel at the incredible variety and creativity of the troll dolls, from the classic Dam dolls of the 1960s to the modern-day Good Luck Trolls. Learn about the history and cultural significance of these beloved toys, and even create your own troll doll to take home as a souvenir.

The Troll Hole Museum is a must-see destination for anyone with a love for nostalgia, quirky collections, or just plain fun. It's a place that will bring a smile to your face, awaken your inner child, and leave you with a newfound appreciation for the power of imagination and play.

2. The Hartman Rock Garden (Springfield, OH)

Discover a hidden gem of folk art at The Hartman Rock Garden in Springfield, Ohio. This incredible outdoor sculpture garden, created by local artist Ben Hartman during the Great Depression, features over 50 intricate miniature castles, churches, and other structures made entirely from small rocks, pebbles, and found objects.

Wander through the winding paths and marvel at the incredible detail and craftsmanship of each tiny building, from the soaring spires of the medieval castle to the delicate arches of the Roman temple. Learn about the inspiring story of Ben Hartman and his tireless dedication to creating beauty and joy in the face of adversity.

The Hartman Rock Garden is a must-see destination for anyone with a love for art, history, or just plain perseverance. It's a place that will awaken your sense of wonder, challenge your notions of what is possible, and leave you with a newfound appreciation for the incredible power of the human spirit.

101 Bizarre, Quirky and Totally Fun Adventures in ...

3. The Topiary Park (Columbus, OH)

Step into a world of green magic at The Topiary Park in Columbus, Ohio. This stunning seven-acre park, located in the heart of the city, features an incredible living sculpture garden that recreates Georges Seurat's famous painting "A Sunday Afternoon on the Island of La Grande Jatte" entirely out of topiary plants.

Stroll through the park and marvel at the incredible artistry and skill of the topiary artists, who have carefully shaped and trimmed over 50 individual topiaries to create a stunningly lifelike replica of the painting, complete with people, animals, and even boats on the "river" of grass.

The Topiary Park is a must-see destination for anyone with a love for art, nature, or just plain whimsy. It's a place that will transport you to another world, awaken your sense of wonder and delight, and leave you with a newfound appreciation for the incredible creativity and beauty of the natural world.

4. The House of Trash (Philo, OH)

Get ready to rethink your definition of "trash" at Blue Rock Station, also known as the House of Trash in Philo, Ohio. This unique creation features an incredible collection of over 10,000 pieces of "trash" that have been creatively repurposed into art, furniture, and other functional objects.

Marvel at the incredible ingenuity and creativity of the artists, who have transformed everything from old car parts to discarded plastic bottles into stunning works of art. Learn about the importance of recycling and sustainability, and even take home a one-of-a-kind upcycled souvenir from the gift shop.

The House of Trash is a must-see destination for anyone with a love for art, environmentalism, or just plain outside-the-box thinking. It's a place that will challenge your assumptions, awaken your sense of possibility, and leave you with a newfound appreciation for the incredible potential of the things we throw away.

5. Corn Henge (Dublin, OH)

The Field of Corn, or "Corn Henge" (as the locals call it), is a must-see public art installation in Dublin, Ohio. Commissioned by the Dublin Arts Council and completed in 1994, this unique display features 109 concrete ears of corn standing upright in a grassy field, accompanied by two rows of Osage-orange trees. The installation serves as a tribute to Sam Frantz, an inventor of several hybrid corn species, and a reminder of Dublin's agricultural heritage.

Visitors to the Sam and Eulalia Frantz Park, where the installation is located, can expect to see the 6-foot-tall (1.8 m) concrete ears of corn arranged in rows, with each ear rotated in different directions to create the illusion of uniqueness. The ears represent Corn Belt Dent Corn, a double-cross hybrid variety, and were cast using three different molds at a precast concrete manufacturer in Dalton, Georgia. Each ear weighs an impressive 1,500 lb (680 kg).

The Field of Corn has become a beloved and popular piece of public art in this central Ohio community, receiving numerous "Best of Columbus" honors by readers of Columbus Monthly Magazine since 2008. Tourists visiting Dublin should not miss the opportunity to explore this one-of-a-kind art installation and learn about the city's agricultural roots through the informative signs located near the Osage orange trees on the west side of the park.

6. The World's Largest Cuckoo Clock (Sugarcreek, OH)

Take a trip back in time at The World's Largest Cuckoo Clock in Sugarcreek, Ohio. This massive timepiece, standing over 23 feet tall and weighing over 3,000 pounds, is a stunning example of the intricate craftsmanship and mechanical ingenuity of traditional cuckoo clocks.

Watch in awe as the giant cuckoo emerges from the clock every hour on the hour, accompanied by music and dancing figurines. Learn about the history and cultural significance of cuckoo clocks, and even take a peek inside the clock's inner workings to see how it all comes together.

The World's Largest Cuckoo Clock is a must-see destination for anyone with a love for timekeeping, engineering, or just plain oversized novelties. It's a place that will make you smile, marvel, and appreciate the incredible skill and dedication of the artisans who keep this classic tradition alive.

7. The Pencil Sharpener Museum (Logan, OH)

Sharpen your sense of wonder at The Pencil Sharpener Museum in Logan, Ohio. This one-of-a-kind museum, housed in the historic Logan Post Office, features an incredible collection of over 3,400 pencil sharpeners from around the world, spanning over 100 years of history.

Marvel at the incredible variety and creativity of the sharpeners, from classic hand-cranked models to modern electric ones, and everything in between. Learn about the history and evolution of pencil sharpeners, and even try your hand at sharpening a pencil on some of the antique models.

The Pencil Sharpener Museum is a must-see destination for anyone with a love for quirky collections, vintage technology, or just plain everyday objects. It's a place that will sharpen your mind, tickle your funny bone, and leave you with a newfound appreciation for the simple things in life.

8. The Chateau Laroche (Loveland, OH)

Step into a medieval fantasy land at The Chateau Laroche in Loveland, Ohio. This stunning castle, also known as the Loveland Castle, was single-handedly built by World War I veteran and medieval enthusiast Harry D. Andrews over the course of 50 years.

Explore the castle's winding stone passages, soaring towers, and lush gardens, all painstakingly crafted by hand using local river rocks and homemade bricks. Learn about the incredible story of Harry Andrews and his lifelong quest to bring his vision of a medieval castle to life.

The Chateau Laroche is a must-see destination for anyone with a love for history, architecture, or just plain dream-chasing. It's a place that will transport you to another time and place, awaken your sense of wonder and possibility, and leave you with a newfound appreciation for the power of one person's vision and determination.

* * *

101 Bizarre, Quirky and Totally Fun Adventures in ...

From the whimsical wonders of The Troll Hole Museum to the medieval magic of The Chateau Laroche, Ohio's quirky attractions offer a glimpse into the state's rich history, diverse culture, and endlessly creative spirit. These eight adventures are just a small taste of the many oddities and amusements waiting to be discovered in the Buckeye State.

Whether you're a lifelong resident or a curious traveler, these unique experiences will leave you with unforgettable memories and a newfound appreciation for Ohio's one-of-a-kind character. So grab your sense of adventure, your camera, and your love for the unexpected, and set out to explore the weird and wonderful side of Ohio. You never know what amazing discoveries await you in the heart of the Midwest!

Chapter 12

South Dakota: Mount Rushmore State Marvels and Mysteries

South Dakota, known as the Mount Rushmore State, is a land of stunning natural beauty, rich history, and a surprising array of quirky and captivating attractions. From the towering peaks of the Black Hills to the vast prairies of the Great Plains, South Dakota is filled with hidden gems waiting to be discovered. But beyond the famous faces of Mount Rushmore and the rugged landscapes of the Badlands lies a world of bizarre, fun, and utterly unforgettable experiences that will leave you amazed and amused.

Join us as we embark on a journey through eight of the most incredible and unusual adventures the Mount Rushmore State has to offer. Get ready to embrace your inner explorer and uncover the marvels and mysteries that make South Dakota truly one-of-a-kind.

***

1. The World's Only Corn Palace (Mitchell, SD)

Feast your eyes on a palace fit for a kernel king at The Corn Palace in Mitchell, South Dakota. This unique building, originally constructed in 1892, is entirely decorated with colorful murals and designs made from corn, grains, and native grasses.

Each year, the palace is stripped down and redecorated with a new theme, requiring over 500,000 ears of corn in 12 different colors. Step inside to marvel at the intricate corn murals, depicting scenes from South Dakota history, culture, and agriculture.

The Corn Palace is a must-see destination for anyone with a love for arts and crafts, agriculture, or just plain quirky Americana. It's a place that will make you smile, learn, and appreciate the incredible creativity and resourcefulness of the South Dakota spirit.

2. Cosmos Mystery Area (Rapid City, SD)

The Cosmos Mystery Area is a family-friendly attraction that offers a unique and unforgettable experience for visitors of all ages. The main highlight is the 40-minute cabin tour, which showcases the mysterious phenomena discovered in the area. After the tour, visitors can enjoy various activities, such as digging for treasures in the geode mine, cooling down with some ice cream, and browsing the extensive gift shop filled with souvenirs from the Cosmos Mystery Area and the Black Hills of South Dakota.

The Cosmos Mystery Area was accidentally discovered in 1952 by two college boys who were searching for the perfect spot to build a summer cabin in the Black Hills. As they explored the area, they stumbled upon a mysterious world that defied explanation. Intrigued by their findings, the boys decided to camp out and investigate the odd phenomena further.

Upon realizing that their discovery would be of interest to the general public, the boys began to fix up the cabin, making it safe for visitors to experience the demonstrations that showcase the area's peculiar characteristics. Today, the Cosmos Mystery Area stands as a testament to their curiosity and dedication, offering visitors a glimpse into the mysterious world they uncovered in the Black Hills. So what is the mystery? Visit and find out!

3. The Dinosaur Park (Rapid City, SD)

Step back in time to the age of the dinosaurs at The Dinosaur Park in Rapid City, South Dakota. This classic roadside attraction, built in 1936 by the Works Progress Administration, features seven life-size concrete dinosaur sculptures perched atop a hill overlooking the city.

Climb up to the top of the hill to get up close and personal with the giant T-Rex, Triceratops, and other prehistoric beasts. Take in the breathtaking views of the Black Hills and the surrounding prairie, and learn about the fascinating history and geology of the region.

The Dinosaur Park is a must-see destination for anyone with a love for history, science, or just plain old-fashioned roadside kitsch. It's a place that will awaken your inner child, spark your imagination, and leave you with a newfound appreciation for the ancient wonders that once roamed the Earth.

4. The Mammoth Site (Hot Springs, SD)

Discover the hidden world of the Ice Age at The Mammoth Site in Hot Springs, South Dakota. This unique archaeological site, located on the site of a former sinkhole, is the world's largest known concentration of mammoth remains.

Take a guided tour of the active dig site and watch as paleontologists uncover the bones of these ancient giants, perfectly preserved in the sinkhole's layers of sediment. Learn about the incredible history and ecology of the mammoths, and even touch a real mammoth tooth or tusk.

The Mammoth Site is a must-see destination for anyone with a love for science, history, or just plain awe-inspiring natural wonders. It's a place that will transport you back in time, challenge your understanding of the world, and leave you with a newfound respect for the incredible creatures that once walked the Earth.

5. The Geographic Center of the Nation Monument (Belle Fourche, SD)

The Geographic Center of the Nation Monument is a must-see attraction for tourists visiting western South Dakota. Located in the town of Belle Fourche, this monument celebrates the central point of the United States. Although the actual geographic center is situated on private property, the National Geodetic Survey designated Belle Fourche as the closest town, making it the perfect spot for this impressive monument.

Standing 21 feet in diameter, the Geographic Center of the Nation Monument is an imposing sight that attracts visitors from far and wide. Its location next to the Center of the Nation Visitor Center and the Tri-State Museum makes it easily accessible year-round, ensuring that tourists can visit this iconic landmark regardless of the season.

Don't forget to snap a selfie with the monument as your backdrop! The Geographic Center of the Nation Monument provides a unique and memorable photo opportunity that you won't want to miss.

Whether you're a geography enthusiast, a history buff, or simply looking for a fun and interesting stop on your South Dakota adventure, this monument is sure to leave a lasting impression.

6. The Petrified Wood Park (Lemmon, SD)

Take a walk through a prehistoric forest at The Petrified Wood Park in Lemmon, South Dakota. This unique park, built in the 1930s by local rock enthusiast Ole S. Quammen, features over 100 structures made entirely out of petrified wood, including a castle, a wishing well, and even a petrified wood locomotive.

Wander through the park's winding paths and marvel at the incredible colors and textures of the petrified wood, which dates back over 60 million years to the time of the dinosaurs. Learn about the fascinating process of petrification and the ancient history of the region.

The Petrified Wood Park is a must-see destination for anyone with a love for geology, history, or just plain natural beauty. It's a place that will transport you to another time and place, awaken your sense of won-

101 Bizarre, Quirky and Totally Fun Adventures in ...

der, and leave you with a newfound appreciation for the incredible treasures hidden beneath the Earth's surface.

7. The Wall Drug Store (Wall, SD)

Step back in time to the heyday of the American road trip at The Wall Drug Store in Wall, South Dakota. This iconic roadside attraction, founded in 1931, started as a small pharmacy offering free ice water to weary travelers and has since grown into a sprawling complex of shops, restaurants, and attractions.

Explore the store's many quirky and kitschy delights, from the giant jackalope statue to the animatronic T-Rex. Enjoy a famous Wall Drug doughnut or a 5-cent cup of coffee, and marvel at the incredible collection of Western art and memorabilia.

The Wall Drug Store is a must-see destination for anyone with a love for Americana, nostalgia, or just plain road trip fun. It's a place that will transport you back to a simpler time, awaken your sense of adventure, and leave you with a smile on your face and a spring in your step.

8. Chapel in the Hills (Rapid City, SD)

Chapel in the Hills is a stave church located near Rapid City, South Dakota, United States. The church is an exact replica of the Borgund stave church in Norway, which was built around the year 1150 and is considered the most completely preserved stave church still standing in Norway. The Norwegian Department of Antiquities provided blueprints of the Borgund church for the construction of the Chapel in the Hills, and the woodcarvings were created by Norwegian woodcarver Erik Fridstrøm and Rapid City resident Helge Christiansen.

The Chapel in the Hills was dedicated on July 6, 1969, as the home for the radio ministry of Lutheran Vespers, with hosts such as Richard A. Jensen broadcasting nationwide from this location in the Black Hills. The church is a special ministry of the South Dakota Synod of the Evangelical Lutheran Church in America.

Visitors to the Chapel in the Hills can also explore an authentic log cabin museum built in 1876 by Edward Nielsen, a Norwegian immigrant gold prospector from Hole,

101 Bizarre, Quirky and Totally Fun Adventures in ...

Ringerike, Norway. Additionally, there is a stabbur, a grass-roofed house, that serves as the visitor center and gift shop, adding to the unique Norwegian cultural experience for tourists visiting the site.

* * *

From the towering dinosaurs of The Dinosaur Park to the quirky charms of The Wall Drug Store, South Dakota's bizarre and beautiful attractions offer a glimpse into the state's rich history, diverse culture, and endlessly surprising spirit. These eight adventures are just a small taste of the many marvels and mysteries waiting to be discovered in the Mount Rushmore State.

Whether you're a lifelong resident or a curious traveler, these unique experiences will leave you with unforgettable memories and a newfound appreciation for South Dakota's one-of-a-kind character. So grab your sense of adventure, your camera, and your love for the unexpected, and set out to explore the weird and wonderful side of South Dakota. You never know what amazing discoveries await you in the heart of the Great Plains!

Chapter 13

Wisconsin: Badger State Wonders and Oddities

Wisconsin, affectionately known as the Badger State, is a land of stunning natural beauty, friendly Midwestern charm, and a delightful array of quirky and captivating attractions. From the shores of Lake Michigan to the rolling hills of the Driftless Area, Wisconsin is filled with hidden gems waiting to be discovered.

But beyond the famous cheese curds and beer culture lies a world of bizarre, fun, and utterly unforgettable experiences that will leave you amazed and amused. Join us as we embark on a journey through eight of the most incredible and unusual adventures the Badger State has to offer. Get ready to embrace your inner explorer and uncover

101 Bizarre, Quirky and Totally Fun Adventures in ...

the wonders and oddities that make Wisconsin truly one-of-a-kind.

* * *

1. The House on the Rock (Spring Green, WI)

Step into a world of unimaginable wonder at The House on the Rock in Spring Green, Wisconsin. This sprawling complex, built by eccentric architect Alex Jordan Jr., features an eclectic collection of art, artifacts, and automated music machines that will leave you speechless.

Explore the house's many themed rooms and exhibits, from the Infinity Room, which extends 218 feet over the valley below, to the world's largest indoor carousel, featuring 269 handcrafted animals. Marvel at the incredible ingenuity and creativity of Jordan's designs, which blend architecture, art, and engineering in truly mind-bending ways.

The House on the Rock is a must-see destination for anyone with a love for the extraordinary, the whimsical, or just plain jaw-dropping spectacles. It's a place that will challenge your perception of reality, awaken your sense of wonder, and leave you with a newfound appreciation for the power of human imagination.

2. The Forevertron (Sumpter, WI)

Witness the world's largest scrap metal sculpture at The Forevertron in Sumpter, Wisconsin. This incredible art installation, created by former salvage yard owner Tom Every (also known as Dr. Evermor), stands 50 feet tall and weighs over 300 tons.

Marvel at the intricate details and sheer scale of the sculpture, which is made entirely out of recycled industrial parts and machinery. Learn about the fascinating backstory of Dr. Evermor, a self-proclaimed "time traveler" who built the Forevertron as a fictional spacecraft to launch himself into the heavens.

The Forevertron is a must-see destination for anyone with a love for outsider art, science fiction, or just plain mind-blowing creativity. It's a place that will spark your imagination, challenge your assumptions about what is possible, and leave you with a sense of awe and wonder.

3. The Trollway (Mount Horeb, WI)

Take a stroll through a magical world of trolls at The Trollway in Mount Horeb, Wisconsin. This charming outdoor attraction features over 15 life-size troll sculptures, each with its own unique personality and backstory.

Explore the village's Main Street and discover the trolls hiding in plain sight, from the friendly "Trollcome to Mount Horeb" sign to the mischievous "Trollway Hitchhiker" looking for a ride. Learn about the fascinating history of Mount Horeb's troll tradition, which dates back to the town's Norwegian heritage.

The Trollway is a must-see destination for anyone with a love for whimsy, folklore, or just plain silly fun. It's a place that will bring a smile to your face, a spring to your step, and a renewed sense of childlike wonder to your heart.

4. The Painted Forest (Valton, WI)

Discover a hidden masterpiece of folk art at The Painted Forest in Valton, Wisconsin.

This incredible work of art, created by German immigrant Ernst Hupeden in the late 19th century, covers the walls and ceiling of a small wooden lodge with intricate murals depicting scenes from American history and mythology.

Step inside the lodge and marvel at the stunning colors, details, and symbolism of Hupeden's paintings, which blend Native American, Biblical, and patriotic themes in a truly unique and captivating way. Learn about the incredible story of Hupeden's life and the dedication and skill that went into creating this remarkable work of art.

The Painted Forest is a must-see destination for anyone with a love for history, art, or just plain hidden gems. It's a place that will transport you back in time, awaken your sense of awe and reverence, and leave you with a newfound appreciation for the power of one man's vision and talent.

5. The Dickeyville Grotto (Dickeyville, WI)

Experience a world of divine inspiration at The Dickeyville Grotto in Dickeyville, Wisconsin. This incredible folk art environment, created by Father Mathias Wernerus in the 1920s and 1930s, features a series of elaborate concrete shrines and structures adorned with colorful stones, shells, and glass.

Explore the grotto's many nooks and crannies, from the towering "Shrine of the Blessed Virgin" to the intricate "Tree of Life" mosaic. Learn about the fascinating story of Father Wernerus and the devotion and artistry that went into creating this awe-inspiring work of faith and beauty.

The Dickeyville Grotto is a must-see destination for anyone with a love for spirituality, creativity, or just plain wonder. It's a place that will fill you with a sense of peace, reverence, and gratitude for the incredible beauty and diversity of human expression.

6. The Jurustic Park (Marshfield, WI)

Step into a world of prehistoric whimsy at The Jurustic Park in Marshfield, Wisconsin. This unique sculpture garden, created by local artist Clyde Wynia, features over 200 incredible metal sculptures of dinosaurs, dragons, and other fantastical creatures.

Wander through the park's winding paths and marvel at the incredible detail and creativity of Wynia's sculptures, which are made entirely out of recycled metal and found objects. Learn about the fascinating story of Wynia's artistic journey and the inspiration behind his quirky and captivating creations.

The Jurustic Park is a must-see destination for anyone with a love for art, humor, or just plain fun. It's a place that will spark your imagination, tickle your funny bone, and leave you with a renewed sense of joy and wonder.

7. World's Largest Six-Pack (La Crosse, WI)

La Crosse, Wisconsin, is home to a unique and eye-catching landmark that pays homage to the city's rich brewing heritage. Located at 3rd St S, La Crosse, WI 54601, the World's Largest Six-Pack is a must-see attraction for both beer enthusiasts and those who appreciate quirky roadside attractions.

This giant six-pack consists of six enormous storage tanks, each meticulously painted to resemble a can of beer. The artwork on the tanks is so detailed and realistic that from a distance, it's easy to mistake them for actual, oversized beer cans. It's a great spot for a selfie.

The World's Largest Six-Pack serves as a tribute to La Crosse's long-standing brewing tradition. The city has been a hub for beer production since the mid-19th century, with numerous breweries calling La Crosse home over the years. The painted storage tanks not only showcase the city's pride in its brewing history but also demonstrate the local community's creativity and sense of humor.

8. The Hodag (Rhinelander, WI)

Go on a quest for the legendary Hodag in Rhinelander, Wisconsin. This mythical creature, a fierce green beast with the head of a frog, the face of an elephant, and the back of a dinosaur, has been a beloved part of Rhinelander's folklore since the late 19th century.

Explore the town's many Hodag-themed attractions, from the larger-than-life Hodag statue downtown to the annual

Hodag Country Festival. Learn about the fascinating history of the Hodag legend and the colorful characters who helped to create and perpetuate it.

The Hodag is a must-see destination for anyone with a love for tall tales, local lore, or just plain quirky fun. It's a place that will capture your imagination, awaken your sense of adventure, and leave you with a newfound appreciation for the power of storytelling and community pride.

* * *

From the mind-bending wonders of The House on the Rock to the legendary lore of The Hodag, Wisconsin's quirky attractions offer a glimpse into the state's rich history, diverse culture, and endlessly creative spirit. These eight adventures are just a small taste of the many wonders and oddities waiting to be discovered in the Badger State.

Whether you're a lifelong resident or a curious traveler, these unique experiences will leave you with unforgettable memories and a newfound appreciation for Wisconsin's one-of-a-kind character. So grab your sense of adventure, your camera, and your

101 Bizarre, Quirky and Totally Fun Adventures in ...

love for the unexpected, and set out to explore the weird and wonderful side of Wisconsin. You never know what amazing discoveries await you in the heart of the Midwest!

Chapter 14

The Road Goes Ever On

Congratulations, adventurous traveler! You've made it to the end of 101 Bizarre, Quirky and Totally Fun Adventures in the Midwest. By now, your head is probably spinning with all the incredible, wacky, and downright unforgettable attractions you've discovered within these pages. From world's things to enchanting art, from the bizarre to the legendary, the Midwest has no shortage of quirky and captivating destinations to explore.

But as any seasoned traveler knows, the end of one journey is just the beginning of another. The Midwest is a vast and varied region, with countless hidden gems and offbeat attractions waiting to be discovered. Whether you've checked off every destina-

101 Bizarre, Quirky and Totally Fun Adventures in ...

tion in this book or just a handful, there's always more to see, more to do, and more to experience in America's Heartland.

Be sure to visit our **Midwest travel blog** at: **www.jackandkitty.com** - we pubish new articles daily and it's an excellent (and totally free) resource for travelers. You also might get a kick out of our daily podcast - **Travel with Jack and Kitty**. Listen on your favorite podcast player or app.

So as you close this book and set off on your own Midwestern adventure, remember to keep your sense of wonder, your spirit of curiosity, and your love for the unexpected alive and well. Don't be afraid to take the road less traveled, to explore the small towns and back roads, and to embrace the quirky and bizarre wherever you find it. You never know what kind of amazing discoveries and unforgettable memories await you just around the bend.

As you embark on your journey, we wish you safe travels, happy trails, and a hearty dose of Midwestern hospitality. May your adventures be filled with laughter, joy, and a newfound appreciation for the wonderfully wacky side of America's Heartland. And may you always remember that

Travel with Jack and Kitty

the road goes ever on, leading you to new and exciting destinations, both in the Midwest and beyond.

So here's to you, intrepid traveler. Have fun discovering the weird and wonderful in the world around us. May you always find your way back to the Midwest, where quirky, bizarre, and totally fun adventures never cease to amaze and inspire.

Happy travels. We'll see you down the road!

Jack and Kitty

Traveling to the Heartland?

Check out Jack and Kitty's Midwest Travel Guidebooks!

Wisconsin's Best:
365 Unique Adventures

Minnesota's Best:
365 Unique Adventures

Iowa's Best:
365 Unique Adventures

Available in bookstores everywhere and at JackAndKitty.com

Midwest Travel Tips

Listen to Jack and Kitty's Fun Daily Podcast!

Join Emmy Award winning travel experts Jack and Kitty as they share the best of the Midwest. From culture to cuisine, history to mystery, you'll learn something about the heartland of America every day of the week! Listen to new episodes of this funny and lighthearted educational podcast every morning at 6:00 AM CST.

Subscribe on your favorite podcast app like: Spotify, Apple Podcasts, YouTube Music, Audible, Amazon Music, Pandora, iHeartRadio, Castbox, Pocket Casts, and Radio Public.

Available everywhere you listen! Info: JackAndKitty.com/Podcast

New from Jack and Kitty's Feel-Good Stories...

Feel-Good Stories for Dog Lovers

Feel-Good Stories about Animals

Christmas Feel-Good Stories: Holidays in the Heartland

Valentine's Day Feel-Good Stories

Available in bookstores everywhere and at JackAndKitty.com

About the Authors

Jack and Kitty Norton are Emmy Award winning authors and Midwest travel experts. They have spent a lifetime on the road: as traveling musicians, documentary filmmakers and television producers.

They now focus on building the **"Travel with Jack and Kitty"** brand which includes a travel blog, guidebooks, podcast and videos. Jack and Kitty offer travelers fun and quirky things to do in Minnesota and the Midwest.

With their branded book series, **"Jack and Kitty's Feel-Good Stories"** they present heartwarming tales from the heartland of America.

High school sweethearts turned married soulmates, the fun-loving couple lives in the small college town of Winona, Minnesota and would love to have you over for some tater tot hotdish.

Connect with Jack and Kitty

We love sharing fun things to do in the Midwest! Please connect with us online for lots more fun travel tips and tricks to make the most out of your time in the Heartland.

Links

Travel Blog
Our travel blog is updated daily with articles and fun resources to help make your next trip awesome! Find it at:
JackAndKitty.com

Travel with Jack and Kitty: The Podcast
From culture to cuisine, history to mystery, you'll learn something about the heartland of America every day of the

101 Bizarre, Quirky and Totally Fun Adventures in ...

week! Find it on your favorite podcast app or online at:
JackAndKitty.com/Podcast

Travel Videos on YouTube
Do we love making travel vids for Youtube? You betcha! Join us for video tours, hidden gems and history lessons all about the Midwest! Subscribe at:
YouTube.com/@JackAndKitty

Facebook
https://www.facebook.com/jackandkittyxo

Instagram
https://www.instagram.com/jackandkittyxo

TikTok
https://www.tiktok.com/@jackandkitty.com

Twitter
https://twitter.com/jackandkittyxo

Suggestion or Correction?

Travel with Jack and Kitty

Do you have a suggestion for a fun place to include in future editions of this book? Maybe you'd like us to write a blog article or make a video about a neat place in the Midwest? We'd love to hear your ideas!

Also, we'll try to keep this book as up-to-date as possible, but if you have a correction or tip, please email us at: **tatertot@jackandkitty.com** - we appreciate your help and look forward to connecting with you!

Copyright © 2024 by Travel with Jack and Kitty (Jack Norton, Kitty Norton)

All rights reserved.

No portion of this book may be reproduced in any form without written permission from the publisher or author, except as permitted by U.S. copyright law.

This publication is designed to provide accurate and authoritative information in regard to the subject matter covered. It is sold with the understanding that neither the author nor the publisher is engaged in rendering legal, investment, accounting or other professional services. While the publisher and author have used their best efforts in preparing this book, they make no representations or warranties with respect to the accuracy or completeness of the contents of this book and specifically disclaim any implied warranties of merchantability or fitness for a particular purpose. No warranty may be created or extended by sales representatives or written sales materials. The advice and strategies contained herein may not be suitable for your situation. You should consult with a professional when appropriate. Neither the publisher nor the author shall be liable for any loss of profit or any other commercial damages, including but not limited to special, incidental, consequential, personal, or other damages.

Book Cover by Travel with Jack and Kitty.

1st edition, 2024

www.ingramcontent.com/pod-product-compliance
Lightning Source LLC
Chambersburg PA
CBHW051757310725
30421CB00020B/1230